D0977553

"THE MOST

EFFECTIVE

ORGANIZATION

IN THE U.S."

"THE MOST EFFECTIVE ORGANIZATION IN THE U.S."

LEADERSHIP SECRETS OF THE SALVATION ARMY

ROBERT A. WATSON

and

BEN BROWN

CROWN
BUSINESS
NEW YORK

Copyright © 2001 by The Salvation Army National Corporation

All rights reserved. No part of this book may be reproduced or transmitted in
any form or by any means, electronic or mechanical, including photocopying,
recording, or by any information storage and retrieval system, without permis-
sion in writing from the publisher.

Published by Crown Business, New York, New York.
Member of the Crown Publishing Group.

Random House, Inc. New York, Toronto, London, Sydney, Auckland
www.randomhouse.com

CROWN BUSINESS is a trademark and the Rising Sun colophon
is a registered trademark of Random House, Inc.

Printed in the United States of America

Design by Meryl Sussman Levavi/Digitext

Library of Congress Cataloging-in-Publication Data is available upon request.

ISBN 0-609-60869-X

10 9 8 7 6 5 4 3 2 1

First Edition

For my mother, Verdie Watson Heinz.

During the final stages of writing this book, my mother passed away—or as we say in The Salvation Army, she was "promoted to glory." Just days before her death, in her nursing home in New Jersey, she helped pack Easter baskets for needy children. Because of the profound impact of her life on so many, including me and my siblings, I want to dedicate this book to her memory and ministry.

She was a great example of "the Army spirit."

ACKNOWLEDGMENTS

This book began with an idea from Joel Fishman and Kevin Lang. As the project's original literary agents, Joel and Kevin brought the coauthors together and represented their efforts through two of the three years it took to make this book a reality. This is their book as much as it is anyone's.

This is also Peter Drucker's book, though he would decline to take any more credit for inspiring us than for inspiring just about everyone else with even a passing interest in organizational theory over the last half-century. We hope we have helped to validate his interest in The Salvation Army and to justify the time he spent with us. And it goes without saying that he shouldn't be held accountable for our lapses as students of his theories.

To focus the wide-ranging ambitions of the manuscript we were blessed with the skills of Crown Business editor John Mahaney, who lent his enthusiasm to the project from our first meeting and helped us refine and enliven our message on just about every page. Jane Dystel and Miriam Goderich of the Jane Dystel Literary Agency represented the authors in the crucial final stages of manuscript preparation and publication.

Of course, this project would have been inconceivable without the men and women of The Salvation Army—the volunteers, employees, and soldiers, as well as the officers—who approached this project with the same giving perspective they bring to other parts of their lives. Time after time, they laid aside pressing business to share their experiences and explain their programs. Some are featured in these pages. Many more contributed to our efforts with no expectation of recognition. They are the real foot soldiers of the Army, working faithfully and with compassion day after day in the trenches of human need.

Our inspiration was the example of our financial supporters across the country who "invest" in the Army as confidently as they might in any business. From those who put a quarter in a Christmas kettle to Joan Kroc, who committed more than $80 million, these are our "share holders" and "trustees."

We should pay tribute to some of the first national journalists to see the power of the theme we developed in these pages: Susan Lee and Ashley Ebeling wrote the authoritative piece in the April 20, 1998, issue of *Forbes* magazine that sparked some of our first discussions about a business book.

Although this was clearly the project of his predecessor as national commander, Commissioner John Busby championed this effort from the moment he took office. And among our cheerleaders and resource providers at the Army's National Headquarters over the last three years were Lt. Colonel Paul Bollwahn, National Social Services Secretary; Lt. Colonel Tom Jones, head of the National Communications and Development Department; Lt. Colonel Marlene Chase, National Editor in Chief and Literary Secretary; Colonel Thomas C. Lewis, National Chief Secretary; and Major George Hood, Assistant National Community Relations and Development Secretary.

Our efforts were encouraged and supported by the Army's four territorial commanders: Commissioners Joe Noland, Lawrence R. Moretz, Raymond A. Cooper, and David Edwards. And the 40 divisional commanders that have taken our message to the frontlines.

Along the way we benefited greatly from the counsel of wise leaders from business and government. Some we featured as prominent examples in these chapters. But many others influenced us more than they know. General Colin L. Powell, whose interest in the work of the Army and efforts on behalf of youth and the dispossessed of the world are sources of great inspiration, was among the first to support our idea. His personal encouragement was a factor in the commitment necessary to see this project through.

In addition to his remarkable and visionary leadership as chairman of our National Advisory Board for three years, Steve Reinemund has been a source of continuing encouragement and blessing. He is one of those corporate leaders who believes in the message we have to convey. In an early meeting with Steve just before he was named chairman and CEO of Pepsico, he encouraged us to set high expectations. What business people need, Steve told us, is not just another list of ways to be better managers but something that addresses head-on the fundamental need for human beings, including human beings who run companies and manage other people, to put meaning in their lives. So we owe to Steve the inspiration for our opening, goal-setting paragraphs: This book is about the meaning of life.

Donald V. Fites, recently retired chairman and CEO of Caterpillar and current chairman of the Army's National Advisory Board, lent his knowledge and enthusiasm from day one. And we have also drawn from the rich experience of valued friends like B. Franklin Skinner, H. Ross Perot, Edsel Ford II, Marlene Klotz Collins, Kurt Weishaupt, and Robert Byers.

Charles Brewer and the founders of *Fast Company* magazine had much to do with our early thinking, even though they might not be aware of it.

Dr. Joseph Beckham of Florida State University, a long-time friend and an expert on the literature of leadership, helped anchor us in theories of contemporary management. And Charles Jimenez turned his Tampa home into a temporary base for research and writing. The first pages of the first draft of this book began on Charlie's dining room table, and the final edits were accomplished in the same place.

Throughout this endeavor, the authors have been blessed by the partnership of our wives and soul mates—Alice Watson and Christine Gardinier. Alice spent hundreds of hours at the computer, as well as lending wisdom and counsel from her four decades of experience as an Army officer. Christine, who for 30 years has forgiven the distractions and the wild enthusiasms of a writer husband, provided—again—unfailing patience and encouragement.

The Watson adult children—Robert, Carol, and Charles—indulged their parents' preoccupation with this project and not only listened attentively to ideas at every stage but also offered valuable suggestions and perspectives we couldn't have otherwise hoped for. For all this help, for all this loving support, we are humble and grateful beyond measure.

COMMISSIONER ROBERT A. WATSON
BEN BROWN

CONTENTS

INTRODUCTION

My motivation for writing this book began during my years as National Commander of The Salvation Army in the United States. During that time, I sensed a growing curiosity in the business sector about our mission and management model, about the scope of our services, and about a track record of success that inspires the public to support us so generously.

People are fascinated when they learn about the breadth and diversity of our efforts and how much support we get from Americans, whether it's a child's quarter dropped into a red kettle at Christmas or an $80 million gift from Joan Kroc, the widow of McDonald's founder Ray Kroc. And there have been recurring themes in recent interviews and articles about us.

In April of 1998, after interviewing my wife Alice and me and researching Salvation Army approaches, *Forbes* magazine published an article that may have surprised people who had never considered our work in a business context. Readers may have been especially intrigued by Dr. Peter F.

Drucker's earlier assessment, repeated in that *Forbes* story, that The Salvation Army is "the most effective organization in the U.S."

It would never occur to us to make that claim for ourselves. It's not our style. But getting such an endorsement from the most respected management expert in the world inspired us to consider what we do from a slightly new angle. We should be prepared, we thought, to answer the questions business leaders might ask as they learned about our work and heard Dr. Drucker's famous assessment of our success: How do we do what we do with such a small core of officer/managers? And how have we managed to do it for so long when so many other organizations with similar ambitions have come and gone?

The curiosity of others inspired me to think about these issues for myself. And the exercise has been fascinating. It has deepened my belief in the mission of this movement, which I love and to which I have gladly given my life. And it has enhanced my appreciation for our faithful supporters.

It has also reinforced my strong conviction that we must never take that sacred trust for granted. We must always be mission-driven. Regardless of inevitable changes in the specific needs of the people we serve or in the methods we discover to serve them, our purpose remains fixed and inviolate. We proclaim it in the Mission Statement we prominently display on Army publications and in our offices and meeting rooms across the country:

> The Salvation Army, an international movement, is an evangelical part of the universal Christian Church.
>
> Its message is based on the Bible. Its ministry is motivated by the love of God. Its mission is to preach the gospel of Jesus Christ and to meet human needs in His name without discrimination.

Our mission is both a direct reflection of our faith and a promise of performance. We expect to be held accountable for it in every decision we make, every project we become involved in.

It is derived from scripture. We believe the Christian life, as taught and modeled by Jesus himself, can be encapsulated in two charges from scripture. One is "Go ye therefore, and teach all nations, baptizing them in the name of the Father, and of the Son, and of the Holy Ghost." (Matthew 28:19, KJV) These words of Jesus, contained in His last pronouncement to His disciples before He ascended into heaven, articulate Christians' evangelical obligations.

The other admonition is from the Biblical account of the Good Samaritan. Speaking of our responsibility to serve the hungry, the thirsty, the naked, the sick, and other broken people, Jesus said: "Inasmuch as ye have done it unto one of the least of these my brethren, ye have done it unto me." (Matthew 25:40, KJV)

Our "theology of service" is built on that two-part foundation. In the following chapters, we'll talk in detail about how we organize ourselves with that dual responsibility in mind. And if you want to know more about The Salvation Army Doctrines that give rise to our convictions, you can read them in the notes at the end of the book. What's worth stressing right now is this: We don't consider the two aspects of our mission, to preach and to serve, as separate from one another. We don't serve people who are hurting only to preach to them. And we don't preach without offering the example of service without discrimination. To us, the two obligations are inseparable.

Some like to call it our holistic ministry—soup, soap, and salvation. But no matter how it's characterized, this integrated ministry of religion and social work is still a distinguishing mark of the Army, even in this information age.

The idea of this book may have come late in my life, but the first seeds were sown many years ago when I was a boy in the small town of Goldsboro, North Carolina. That's where my family first met The Salvation Army.

I was one of six children in a poor family with an alcoholic father and a stress-worn mother. It was near the end of the Great Depression, and my mother was desperate for food, clothes, and shoes for her small children. Her hope was strained, but her faith was strong. She was rock-solid in her resolve to keep her family together and to pray for spiritual strength for her husband. So having no place else to turn, and probably sensing the empathy of caring Salvation Army people, she summoned the courage to ask the Army for help.

The donated clothes were not always a perfect fit and sometimes out of date, but we were mighty grateful for the help. My mother was very innovative in preparing filling meals with some of the donated foods the Army gave us. We could sense new hope and optimism in our humble home. We were poor, but we were bound together with a very strong bond of love and determination. Mother showed a wonderful blend of grace and grit. Somehow, we knew we could make it with God's help . . . and with the Army's.

It wasn't long before the officers in charge of the Army in that small North Carolina town began to discover ways in which crisis intervention could be turned into longer term support for our family. They were able to arrange part-time employment for my mother at the Army, involving her in activities that served others while also helping us. All the while, the encouragement and spiritual nurture my mother received at the Army greatly strengthened her faith in God and brought increased stability to the family.

All six children became actively involved in Army youth programs, which were character-building and life-changing. In fact, when I was about eight years old, in a Salvation Army after-school craft and recreation program, the first sparks of spiritual awakening began to flicker in my young heart and mind when I was introduced to that wonderful Bible promise in John 1:12: "But as many as received Him, to them gave He power to become the sons of God, even to them that believe on His name."

That was a defining moment in my life. We played in bands, took part in sports and recreation programs, and, like our mother, experienced the joy of helping others. Those years planted in our hearts the seeds of desire to pursue full-time ministry in this people-helping movement. To my mother's deep satisfaction, all six of her children subsequently became Salvation Army officers. Since that first contact with the Army at a time of desperation, the hope, help, and healing that came has had a divine rippling effect through two more generations.

Our father and his twin brother had been orphaned by the deaths of both parents by the time they were twelve. It is easier now to understand how the numbing effect of alcohol could seem to be an attractive antidote to the confusion, fears, and worries of such a young man. Especially a father of six, at a time when job opportunities were so scarce. No wonder my father would sometimes seek the company of other men with their bottles in a low patch of ground in Goldsboro with tall weeds and grass called "Buzzard's Roost." There, they would commiserate with each other as they drank themselves into oblivion.

Now, fast-forward just over fifty years from those days of my boyhood. As National Commander of The Salvation Army, I was asked to return to Goldsboro to speak at the Army's Annual Civic Dinner at that town's country club. When I arrived at the dinner, there was an envelope at my place at the head table with a letter from a woman who had been in my third-grade class. She enclosed a class photograph, pointing out in her note that I was the one in the center of the front row smiling.

There I was, in my overalls and white shirt (probably supplied by The Salvation Army) but with no shoes. There was only one other shoeless boy in the picture who was dressed the same as me. I guess we both got our clothes from the Army. After telling the crowd that night that this occasion was my very first visit to the country club, I told them how glad I was that the Army's local budget is now also able to supply shoes!

In the late 1990s, Alice and I were nearing our retirement as The Salvation Army's national leaders. (Married officers in The Salvation Army share a team ministry, though they have their separate responsibilities as well.) I was asked by two retired corporate executives to visit a very high-profile friend of theirs who was in prison for white-collar crimes. Ironically, he was serving time in prison near Seymour Johnson Field in Goldsboro.

I flew to North Carolina from Washington and rented a car. After a very poignant and meaningful visit at the prison, I followed a personal ritual, which has been repeated over the years on the occasional nostalgic visits to Goldsboro. On the way back to the Raleigh-Durham Airport, I drove by "Buzzard's Roost," where I have taken the opportunity at times for a brief "prayer pause" to thank God for His power to help people with addictions and to reflect quietly on the profound impact of the Army on my family.

On one of those occasions, as I sat in my car near this little patch of brokenness, a relatively young man came out of the tall weeds and staggered up the street. It was a jarring juxtaposition of past and present, and he was out of sight before I could collect myself. But I have thought many times since: Was he also struggling with the responsibilities of a large family in crisis? Times have changed, but there are still hurting people who are trying to find their way in this new millennium.

I should point out, with great gratitude, that my mother's prayers for my father were answered before his fatal heart attack at 56 years of age. Recognizing that true and lasting change in a man comes from God and is from the inside out, he made a personal commitment to Jesus Christ before his death. This was one of many experiences over the years that have strengthened my belief that the Army is right on target in its concern for the total person.

Oh, and by the way, the former corporate executive I visited in the prison near Goldsboro? He may soon be released and, by agreement of the courts, will give special service in one of our Salvation Army Harbor Light Centers, as part of a job training team to help people find their "spiritual legs" and a constructive place in society.

Why share all of this with you? What does it have to do with "Leadership Secrets of The Salvation Army"? It is my sincere hope that this book will help readers better understand the motive behind our mission. We want you to know more about the scope of our work but, even more, about the spirit of our witness. What are those timeless principles and core values that make us what we are and help us, in Dr. Drucker's estimation, serve as "the most effective organization in the U.S."? What caused those Salvation Army people in post-Depression Goldsboro, North Carolina, to minister to my family with a sacramental spirit and inspire me and so many others to lives of joyful witness and service?

Thinking about ways to answer questions like that for readers who may not know us well has helped me renew my appreciation for "the Army spirit." When an organization becomes so large and serves so many, there is always the temptation to become so preoccupied with raising money and operating the machinery that you forget your "first love." I am pleased to tell you, however, that there are tens of thousands in the Army family across this country who still find their greatest joy in serving others in the name of Christ in the trenches of human need. This is because we have come to understand that mission is furthered by men and women, not just by money and machinery.

It is the personal commitment of individuals to the mission of the organization that gets the job done. In our case, we think it is not enough to change a man's environment and circumstances, but that we must pray, work, and believe for a change in his heart. This is not just a change in perspective, but a re-ordering of one's priorities and embracing a new set of life principles. It is a spiritual transformation by Christ Himself. William Booth, our founder, believed it was not enough to "take people out of the slums," but that we must "take the slums out of people."

I am convinced that the values and principles that give us purpose and passion are transferable to any company or workplace. This is not about organized religion or denominationalism. It is about what a man or woman has in his or her heart, and how they treat the people around them. It is about living out one's personal values in such a way that the culture in which one lives and works is improved and enriched. This is good for the community—and it is good for business.

So, why should I want to take on the project of this book in my retirement? In large part, it is because of the profound impact of Salvation Army ministries on my life and on my family, and because of the thousands of "trophies of grace," whose lives I have seen changed from the inside out over more than four decades of joyful service in this Army of caring. But there is another reason. It is my hope and prayer that many who read this book will embrace its ideas where they live and work.

That young kid who found Christ and compassion at The Salvation Army so many years ago in North Carolina is now one of the richest retirees in all of Florida. Not rich in material goods, but rather in deep satisfaction for the sacred privilege of ministry through the years and for the exciting opportunities of these days. Among those opportunities is the chance to witness, through these pages, to the power of the Army's purpose, not only in a single life like mine but also in the lives of those who seek to lead organizations they can be proud of. This is The Salvation Army's book. None of the money derived from its sale goes to me personally. But, as always, I continue to share in the abundant profits of the soul from an enterprise sworn to preach the gospel and to serve the hurting of the world.

"The Most Effective Organization in the U.S."? We are humbled and grateful to Dr. Peter Drucker for that appraisal of our work. Such treasured confidence sends us to our knees with the prayer: "God, please make us worthy of such trust!"

Commissioner Robert A. Watson
Retired National Commander
The Salvation Army, U.S.A.

1

THE "BUSINESS" OF THE SALVATION ARMY

We want this to be one of the most important books you'll ever read. It's about the meaning of life.

That's a presumptuous thing to say. But given the mission of The Salvation Army and the needs we sense in the business community, we'd be wasting time if we pretended to be interested in anything less.

What are those needs?

We believe the most important one is for connection with a purpose that's bigger than one person's—or one organization's—material ambitions. It's the need for a set of guiding principles, an anchor when everything is in flux.

It's the only way the world makes sense. People cannot be truly happy or productive over the long haul without acknowledging an overarching purpose for their existence and without working to harmonize their lives' efforts toward realizing it.

People often talk about their work lives, their family lives, and their spiritual lives as if they are distinct sectors they must somehow keep in balance. But that way of looking at things doesn't match up with human experience. We cannot be one person at work, another with friends and family, yet another in our relationship with God.

We are, each of us, one person. We live in one world. We are happiest and most productive when we feel the fragments of our lives moving together toward some meaningful, transcendent purpose.

You don't have to think of yourself as a religious person to believe that. You know it intuitively. And the idea is confirmed by social science research and by clinical psychology, where the aims have long been to encourage a healthy reintegration of those fragments and to support reconnections with principles and with people that give meaning to our lives.

You can pretend this fundamental need for spiritual integration is somehow suspended when you go to work. But your heart tells you otherwise. Boundaries between "the business world" and other worlds in which humans strive are as artificial as the distinctions between our separate private selves.

All organizations are composed of people—people who are managers, partners, investors, workers, and clients—who don't abandon their individual needs and hopes when they come together in a group. You can have the fanciest title, the best salary, the most lavish perquisites. You can enjoy the highest esteem from colleagues and the respect of competitors. But if you don't feel as if your efforts are pointed at something bigger and more important than quarterly earnings or year-end bonuses, if you don't feel you're building a legacy beyond the money you've made or the possessions you've piled up, you're going to be haunted by what's missing in your life.

In our work with clients in Salvation Army programs, we see the pathological dimensions of this gap between what humans need and what they too frequently settle for. Many of those who come to us are lost, desperate. They've tried every-thing to fill the holes in their lives. And while we're committed to helping them face and overcome their problems with alco-hol and drugs or with broken relationships, the real secret of our success is getting them to accept responsibility for inte-grating their hearts, their minds, their souls with transcendent purpose. We help them reconnect.

It's not just those who come to us from the streets, from lives of poverty and deprivation, who need to work through this process. Here, for instance, is how one of our former clients begins his story of re-integration:

> At 3:30 on a Saturday afternoon, Marine One, the military helicopter which carries the President of the United States, lifted off the White House south lawn and headed west over the congested Virginia sprawl. Following Route 236, the chopper passed over The Salvation Army Adult Rehabilita-tion Center, a dormitory for men who could not, or would not, deal with their addiction to alcohol or drugs.
>
> At that precise moment, I was crossing the highway to reach the ARC, where I was a resident. When I heard the familiar sound above, I stopped to absorb the sight and immediately felt deeply ashamed of what I had allowed alco-hol to do to my life. After all, I had been an occasional pas-senger on that very chopper and its larger cousin Air Force One. That heady life of official White House travel and all the perks that went with it rushed to my mind. "How the mighty have fallen," I thought.

This is Bill Rhatican, a former White House official in the Nixon and Ford administrations. After 15 years in and out of various alcohol treatment centers, Rhatican ended up at our residence center in Annandale, Virginia, in 1996.

"When my counselor told me I needed long-term help," he says, "I did not expect the facility to be run by The Salvation

Army. That organization, I knew, was for the homeless and the helpless, the roadside wreckage I had passed so many times on my way to some important meeting. And I still wasn't that sick, or so I thought."

From the other beneficiaries' viewpoints, Rhatican had everything—the high-profile job, the money, the house, the adoring family. They had nothing. Yet there they were, together, going through the same program, suffering the same pains of transition and coming to the same conclusions about what was missing in their lives.

It wasn't any easier an experience for Rhatican than it is for clients who come to us from prisons or homeless shelters. He slipped once, violating the rules of total sobriety while he was in the program, and had to wait for the chance to be readmitted. Yet he stuck it out and was ultimately able to achieve what had been impossible for him in all the other programs he'd tried. He stayed clean and sober.

What he found among the other men in the program, the men who were ahead of him in recognizing and developing their spiritual connection, "was serenity and inner peace," says Rhatican. "What they had, I wanted."

You don't have to be at the end of your rope to want that feeling or to recognize when it's missing in your life. Even if you're living out your dreams of professional achievement and material success, even if you've avoided the most dangerous distractions that threaten health and wreck families, you know when you're not paying enough attention to your spiritual needs. Those needs don't wait on the sidelines while you attend to other business. They demand attention.

The Salvation Army is fueled with the energy generated by this fundamental human drive for spiritual connection. Not only do we get our "customers" that way, we also get our officers, our lay people, our employees, our investors, and our volunteers because of the pull of this need to align ourselves with divine purpose and because of the intrinsic rewards that come with that alignment. We *all* seek serenity and inner peace.

In the coming pages, we're going to explain how we run a $2 billion-a-year, transcontinental organization that serves 30 million customers with a workforce that, by material standards, is vastly underpaid and overworked. The rewards we offer are spiritual ones. Our "pay" is weighted by opportunities for meaningful engagement in challenging arenas and for soul-satisfying service of people in need. And, as we'll demonstrate, that kind of compensation package turns out to be one of the most important ingredients—if not *the* most important ingredient—in building an effective organization.

Can a charity really teach leaders who have to operate in the "real world" of business?

If we truly believe that we all aspire to achieve our best selves beyond mere material concerns and that the organizations we build are simply extensions of our aspirations, then the difference between for-profit organizations and nonprofit ones is about accounting policies, not about proficiency and effectiveness. The bottom line is this: An organization is an organization is an organization.

The Salvation Army assumes principle-centered, people-serving approaches as natural extensions of our faith. We believe that's the way God wants us to live our lives and to relate to others. So that's the way we organize ourselves. But you don't have to take just our word that it will work for any organization. Business consultants and professors who write the most popular books and lead the most influential leadership seminars have come to some of the same conclusions from another direction—by studying what the most successful executives and companies have in common and then converting those commonalities into principles of effectiveness. Prominent among the findings in all those analyses is a correlation between high levels of success and company-wide commitments to purposes that transcend the mere material.

Among the "shattered myths" exposed by their study, write James C. Collins and Jerry I. Porras in *Built to Last: Successful Habits of Visionary Companies,* is that "the most successful companies exist first and foremost to maximize profits."

"Contrary to business school doctrine, 'maximizing shareholder wealth' or 'profit maximization' has not been the dominant driving force or primary objective through the history of visionary companies. . . . Yes, they seek profits, but they're equally guided by a core ideology—core values and sense of purpose beyond just making money."

This is why Collins and Porras say they see "little difference between for-profit visionary companies and nonprofit visionary organizations. . . . [The] essence of what it takes to build an enduring, great institution does not vary."

Why should anyone be surprised when the principles of high-achieving people and organizations turn out to be so similar regardless of how they measure their profits? In the one world in which we all live connected to God and other humans by our common spiritual aspirations, why would we think we'd have to sacrifice our spiritual needs in order to live and work effectively? Isn't it more likely that the opposite is true, that the *only* way we can live and work effectively is to stop ignoring those needs and to begin honoring them?

Peter F. Drucker, perhaps the world's most famous management authority, calls The Salvation Army "by far the most effective organization in the U.S." He didn't say the Army was the most effective religious organization or the most effective nonprofit. He left it unqualified. He said we were the most effective *organization.*

The size, complexity, and diversity of Salvation Army operations mean that many of the challenges we face daily are not all that different from those that any business deals with. And our long-term successes at doing all those things at high levels of efficiency suggest we're onto something. Let's look at our approaches in light of Peter Drucker's five criteria of effectiveness. "No one," he says, "even comes close to [The Salvation Army] in respect to clarity of mission, ability to innovate, measurable results, dedication, and putting money to maximum use."

"Clarity of Mission"

The Salvation Army landed in America on March 10, 1880, fifteen years after it was founded in England by William Booth. The American expeditionary force consisted of eight people, one man and seven women. Their principal assets: Two Salvation Army flags and a conviction they shared with General Booth that the ministry they were called to serve required as much attention to the physical and social conditions of needy people as to their habits of worship—which, as it turns out, was all the founding capital the Army needed.

Three years later, the American branch of The Salvation Army had expanded from New York to New Jersey, Connecticut, Pennsylvania, Indiana, Kentucky, Ohio, Maryland, Massachusetts, Michigan, Missouri, and California. In 1886, Grover Cleveland became the first U.S. president to receive a Salvation Army delegation in the White House. And by the end of World War I, The Salvation Army was a familiar national voice on behalf of the poor and the suffering, with supporters ranging from CEOs of some of the most powerful corporations to volunteers whose worldly goods amounted to not much more than those of the people they served.

As we write this, The Salvation Army is approaching its 121st anniversary in America. We still operate under the same name and offer our "customers" the same dual "product" of salvation and service as we did more than a century ago. Our mission is still "to preach the gospel of Jesus Christ and to meet human needs in His name without discrimination." Think of all the famous enterprises that have faded into oblivion over that same period. Of the firms listed among the original Dow Jones industrials in 1896, only one—General Electric—is still in business.

From near-zero financial resources and a staff of eight in 1880, the Army in the United States has grown into an enterprise with an annual budget exceeding $2 billion and a work force of officers, employees, and volunteers approaching 3.4 million people. That $2 billion figure, says *Forbes* magazine, "understates the value of what it contributes." If you put a number on the extra time contributed by Army staffers and volunteers, said the magazine, "you would get a business that would rank up with the biggest companies in [the] Forbes 500."

The Salvation Army hasn't grown and prospered for more than a century, eclipsing the life spans of most other enterprises, by ignoring practical business considerations. On the contrary. From our beginnings in Victorian England, we have been obligated to develop and refine our business methods so we can make the most of what we have to meet clients' needs and contributors' expectations.

In strictly business terms, our service recipients are our customers and our supporters are investors. Like any other company, the Army has employees to recruit, train, and retain. It has property to manage. It has revenue streams to monitor and costs to control. It has a brand to protect. And it is as determined as any business to generate more money than it spends in order to expand its programs and reach an ever-wider "market" of needy people.

If we and other successful nonprofits have any advantage over many commercial firms, it's that we're not nearly as vulnerable to the distraction so many of the top management gurus warn against—the distraction of short-range earnings demands. It's not that money is not a consideration with us. The fact is, there's never enough money to do what we need to do. We worry constantly about how to raise more and how to spend what we have more efficiently. That will always be an issue. But it's not *the* issue.

We plan strategies, launch and refine programs, recruit people, and evaluate everything we do according to how it relates to preaching the gospel of Jesus Christ and meeting human needs in His name without discrimination. It's really that simple. If a proposal doesn't advance our twofold mission, we're not interested in it. And if something we're involved in begins to compromise either the evangelical or the service aspect of our purpose, we'll bow out.

When I was a divisional officer in the early 1970s, responsible for 30 Salvation Army corps in the Greater New York area, we had a $100,000 New York City–administered contract to feed older people in Harlem. The program had gone on for years with us serving lunches to some 100 people each day. Since so many of these folks came to know one another through these gatherings, it was a community fellowship program as well as a way to get nourishing food to the elderly.

One day, two city officials came to me with a new interpretation of the contract rules. They were uncomfortable with the connection between the service we were providing and our religious mission. They didn't like the fact that our name was prominently displayed in the center—our center, after all— where the lunches took place. They didn't want us to say grace over the meals. And they were alarmed that a Salvation Army officer would join the old people and lead them in some of their favorite hymns. If we wanted to keep getting the money, all that would have to end.

Now, around the country, we have some $250 million in annual contracts with private and public agencies, including governments at all levels. In many places, we find a way to satisfy separation of church and state requirements without compromising our mission. But this particular demand required us to deny who we are. And it was unacceptable.

We refused to make the changes. And the officials pulled the contract and arranged for the lunches to be provided elsewhere.

Interestingly enough, most of the folks we were serving in the Harlem neighborhood refused to go anywhere else. They wanted the program to continue the way it had been. So we found another funding source to keep the fellowship and food going.

Such a laser-like focus on mission has benefits on both the revenue and the cost sides of our operations. People trust us to do what we say we're going to do, so they contribute generously. For eight consecutive years through 2000, The Salvation Army has been at the top of the *Chronicle of Philanthropy*'s annual fund-raising rankings. In 2000, our $1.4 billion total was more than double the amounts donated to runners-up like the YMCA and the Red Cross.

And because they identify so strongly with our mission and track record, people are much more likely to work long hours for low pay or to volunteer time and valuable expertise to Salvation Army projects. That goes for everyone from career Army officers to corporate executives who sit on our regional and national advisory boards.

Motivation by money is just not a factor in The Salvation Army. In an age in which senior executives at major corporations may collect millions in annual salaries, bonuses, and stock options, high-ranking Salvation Army officers responsible for thousands of people and multimillion-dollar budgets work happily for a fraction of those purely financial incentives. In 1999, our last full year of service as co-CEOs of the Army in America, Alice and I together earned slightly less than $74,000, including the taxable benefits of Army-supplied housing and transportation. And we can say with confidence that no executives in America were more richly rewarded—blessed in every sense—by their opportunities and their relationships.

Volunteers, of course, are the ultimate bargain. Many of them take on the responsibilities of staffers, especially when it comes to disaster relief and to seasonal programs. And many of them not only donate their time, they also contribute money. The leaders we attract to our National Advisory Board not only serve without pay, they assume their own travel and hotel expenses when they come to board meetings.

We could never enjoy such support from donors and such selfless commitment from our people if it wasn't absolutely clear what we intended as an organization and if we didn't hold ourselves accountable for acting on those intentions every day.

"Ability to Innovate"

If your mission is to save the world, person by person, community by community, the difference between what you aspire to and what you have to work with makes innovation a survival tactic. Our only chance for success is to achieve multiplier effects from creative approaches.

When we met with Peter Drucker to talk about ideas for this book, the first thing he said to us was this: "I'm going to shock you. You talk about yourself as a charity—and there are surely parts of your operations that fit that description. But I consider you to be venture capitalists.

"Yes, you have some charitable operations, some soup kitchens and so forth. But they are a fairly small part of your programs. A major part of your efforts is in rehabilitation. And that is pure venture capitalism. Your investment in people gets incredible returns."

When someone comes to us for help, we involve them in a

program that doesn't just address their addictions or their employment or relationship problems. We want to awaken in them an awareness of their connection to divine purpose. With that awakening comes an acknowledgment of a need to serve others. So we are recruiting future partners in our long-term mission as we tend to individual short-term needs.

It's not that our clients "owe" us something for our help. It's that they come to realize that helping others is essential to reconnecting with the Spirit and re-assembling the fragments of their lives into a fulfilling whole. When you look at service in that way, as a path to spiritual renewal, you see all kinds of opportunities in even the toughest challenges.

Here's a typical example: We've learned that we get the best results from our drug and alcohol rehabilitation programs if we can keep clients in residence for a period of time. The problem is that there's almost always a shortage of beds, and clients are prone to slip into old habits if they make a decision to go into rehab but have to wait months for an opening in one of our facilities.

In Sarasota, Florida, in 1994, we started the VIP—Voluntary Interim Placement—program to try to involve clients-in-waiting more directly in a network of service. While they wait for housing, they get access to our twelve-step programs, our spiritual counseling, and help with their medical needs—just like the residents.

We noticed that as they became more confident in the process of their own recovery, the VIP clients wanted to do something immediately to apply what they were learning. So we found a way for them to channel those feelings into activities ranging from the Army's disaster relief services to city beautification programs.

As a group, the VIP clients created garden plots so they could grow fresh flowers to put on the tables for the Army's community feeding programs. And they fixed up the homes of low-income residents threatened with eviction because of code violations. In 1995, some of them joined the Army's Hurricane Opal staff, serving food to victims and relief workers. And now, some VIP alums sit on boards working on behalf of the homeless and with community feeding programs.

We can't prove statistically that we would have lost these clients to their alcohol and drug problems if they hadn't gotten involved in the VIP program. But our experience teaches us that backsliding would have been far more likely for many of them.

Adding the VIP approach to our existing network required very little extra investment of time and money. And what we got out of the program was many times what we put in. A venture capitalist's dream.

That's pretty much the way we grow. We see needs as opportunities, problems as future assets. And we plan for multiplier effects. As a result, we've become retailers, with more than 1,600 thrift stores. We're housing providers, with a small city—a population of 65,000 spread across the country—sleeping under Salvation Army roofs every night. And we're social service specialists on an unprecedented scale, delivering everything from instant disaster relief to long-term drug and alcohol rehabilitation.

Besides the services we're most known for, we also provide state-contracted counseling for former prisoners on parole or probation; day care for both children and seniors; community sports and recreation programs; medical services; job training and placement; missing persons services; summer and day camps for kids; and visitations to people in institutions.

Every year our efforts touch the lives of more than 30 million citizens, one in every ten Americans. We have more than 9,000 units of operation and at least one program reaching into every zip code in the country.

We can marshal a work force of 3.4 million people. But

more than 3.3 million of that number are volunteers, including the more than 100,000 lay members—our soldiers—who make up the pool from which future officers are chosen. Of the remainder, 43,000 are employees, whom we categorize separately from the 5,000 men and women who are the uniformed officers most people think of as The Salvation Army.

Many of our employees, of course, hold leadership positions and run some of our most successful programs. But it is up to that group of 5,000 officers to set and enforce standards of performance and principle. It is they who must inspire and lead the millions we need to fulfill even a portion of what our mission promises.

That means we leverage all those programs, provide all those services, with a core management group of just those 5,000. How could we even begin to attempt all that we do without the multiplier effects of innovation?

"Measurable Results"

We have a record of delivering on our promises. The parolees we counsel are less likely to end up back in prison. The homeless we help tend to have a better shot at finding housing and jobs. The addicted we guide through recovery are less likely to return to drugs.

Let's take just a couple of examples. In the San Diego area, Ed Lataille, a Catholic priest and a Ph.D. in clinical psychology, heads our alcohol and drug recovery programs. We've established a strong enough record there that the U.S. Navy has a contract with Dr. Lataille's Salvation Army unit to train Navy personnel in rehabilitation counseling.

National statistics on all rehab programs suggest that only about 20 percent of those who enter such programs remain clean and sober after one year. But Dr. Lataille's studies suggest that our intensive residential treatment and counseling approaches can multiply success rates. In one study of clients who had been admitted to our San Diego transitional housing program over two and a half years, 85 percent were clean and sober at the time of the interview. And of those who had been involved in the program for a year or longer, 78 percent had at least a year of sobriety behind them.

In Chicago, where Claudia Rowland, a daughter of Salvation Army officers and a former Peace Corps volunteer, runs our corrections services, we have a longstanding contract to operate a pre-release transition program for federal prison inmates. Typically, we get them three to six months before they're scheduled to be released to probation or parole. We provide housing and meals, counseling, job placement, and other supports for re-entry into the community.

For the year ending December 31, 2000, Rowland's program served 608 residents in transition. Ninety percent successfully completed the program; 95 percent were employed when they were officially released; and only one percent of the residents were arrested for anything during their time under our supervision.

Of course, you can't quantify everything. We wouldn't want to. The success we have depends more on what's in the hearts of our people and our clients than on what's revealed in statistical reports. But we embrace the idea of accountability. And even in activities that resist quantification, we encourage setting goals that have measurable outcomes.

When we were young officers, Alice and I found it helpful to sit down each fall with leading lay members in our congregation to hammer out goals for the coming year. We tried to make sure each one was specific, measurable, achievable, and mission-related. Each had to have defined steps and timelines for accomplishment. Some goals, of course, had to do with fundraising, marketing, capital improvements, and other concerns of doing business in the community. But we gave priority to those that had to do with programs and services to people.

We had quarterly meetings to monitor progress and to make course corrections. And then, on New Year's Eve, we'd have a well-advertised open meeting to present a Victory Report on the year's achievements and to announce new goals for the coming year.

As we moved up the officer ranks, we used this same concept of setting, monitoring, and celebrating the achievement of measurable goals. Not only is it a good way to keep an organization's efforts moving forward purposefully, it also opens the opportunity for taking inspiration from accomplishments. When you're surrounded by challenges and nagged by unavoidable failures in this or that project, it's important to notice what's working and why. You want everybody associated with your organization to be able to say: "Look, we promised we would do this. And we delivered."

"Dedication"

You wouldn't have to spend much time with one of our volunteers to marvel at the passion they bring to their Army assignments. They are inspired, they say, by what they see working in the lives of our program beneficiaries and by the example of our officers. There's no way to overestimate the power of that example, which is really Christ's example modeled by those of us who have committed our lives to ministry and service.

Frank Skinner, the former chairman and CEO of BellSouth Telecommunications, Inc., is among the longtime friends of the Army who first became involved with us because of being infected with the mission-committed enthusiasm of officers. In the mid-1960s, when he was a rising telecommunications executive in Richmond, Virginia, he agreed "out of courtesy," he says, to meet with a regional Army commander and walked out of the session "with a list of 20 or 30 things to do."

Over the next 35 years, Skinner assisted Army programs and sat on advisory boards. He was chairman of our national board in the late 1980s. There were times, Skinner admits, when the careful, consensus-oriented style of Army management may have run counter to his instincts as a time-pressed, corporate decision-maker. "But through it all," he says, "the Army has always had this wonderful ability to make the most of the sincere dedication of its people.

"These are the most joyous, selfless people I have ever known. You can't be associated with them and not feel it. You'd have to be deaf, dumb, and blind."

We count on that feeling radiating through our lay people, our employees, our clients, and our 3.3 million volunteers. It begins with the absolute mission-commitment of officers, who are trained not only as managers and counselors, but as ordained ministers. Officers sign a covenant, renouncing worldly distractions such as alcohol, drugs, and tobacco and focusing every aspect of our lives on Christ's example of compassion and service.

To avoid the stress of competing careers on officer families, both spouses must be officers. This means that before a married officer candidate can be considered, his or her spouse must agree to enter training as well, and when single officers marry, they have to marry other officers or people who agree to become officers.

Our covenant is life-long. So a Salvation Army officer's retirement from active duty is really just "a change of assignment." In fact, we include retirees in the official total of all Salvation Army officers. The actual breakdown for our officer group in 2000 was a total of 5,326 men and women, divided into 3,697 active and 1,629 retired.

While someone outside our organization might commend

us for making the sacrifices such dedication requires, we see it another way. It's not what we're giving up that drives us and inspires others; it's what we gain in the way of soul-deep fulfillment—that joy that Frank Skinner observes in his Army friends.

One of my favorite examples of the way dedication is contagious and rewarding involves Don Ross, the son of an alcoholic father and one of seven children. When he was beginning his teen years in the early 1950s, he "tumbled into an extended family of loving people" in the Newark, New Jersey, Salvation Army Corps, he says. "While my friends were hanging around street corners and going in and out of jail, I was meeting a lot of caring and very focused adults who showed me that life has a purpose beyond just material gain."

Ross became a junior soldier, then a senior soldier—our designation for dedicated lay people in the congregational life of The Salvation Army from which we take our future leaders. He worked for the Army while he attended New York University. Then he won a fellowship to graduate school at Columbia University and was a dissertation away from his Ph.D. in classics, when he decided on another career path—law. He graduated from law school at the University of Albany, then took a job with General Electric, where he worked for the next 27 years, rising to become general counsel of the company's electrical distribution and control division.

At one point in his career, Ross supervised the acquisition of ten European companies for G.E. and helped knit them together into a $1.5 billion-a-year operation. His quarter-century at G.E. was "very exhilarating," he says. "It was the chance to play for very high stakes, to move among very powerful people. Working at G.E. during those years was a living M.B.A."

Still, during all that time with the company, Ross maintained close ties with the Army, continuing as a lay worker for a local corps in Connecticut. When he got the chance to take early retirement in 2000, he decided to devote the rest of his life to full-time Army service. Now, he's the Army's area services coordinator in Albany, New York.

"I found a profound joy in being a lawyer for General Electric," says Ross. "But at 62, you don't know how many more years of good health you have ahead of you. And I wanted to give the Lord some quality time.

"I saw the chance to launch Chapter 3 in the book of my life. First, it was as a teacher of the classics. Then it was law. Now it's The Salvation Army. A slightly different text, maybe, but the same theme. Once you've had the experience of joy as a Christian, everything you do is part of that joy."

Don Ross's G.E. career made it possible for him and his family to live without financial worries for the rest of his life. In his new job with the Army, he takes no salary and pays his own expenses. No doubt, many of Ross's corporate colleagues would consider that dedication far beyond the call of duty. But he talks mostly about what he's getting out of the deal. When he made the decision to begin Chapter 3, he says, "I said what I wanted was to be filled with the Spirit."

"Putting Money to Maximum Use"

We try hard not to waste a lot of time and money on processes that don't directly serve our programs. Of every dollar we receive, at least 83 cents goes directly to services to people. The other 17 cents fund an infrastructure that supports the programs and our front-line people and that covers the costs of administration and fundraising.

That infrastructure is anything but top-heavy. At National Headquarters in Alexandria, Virginia, for instance, we maintain a staff of less than 100 to oversee operations in four regional territories that extend from Maine to Florida to California to Alaska and the Pacific islands. Almost all the action, the money, the people, and the energy is directed into regions and communities where officers, lay members, employees, and volunteers have hands-on, day-in and day-out relationships with the folks they serve.

The best way to illustrate how we make the most of our resources is to take an example from one project in one city at one time of the year. Our people in Dallas operate a 48,000-square-foot warehouse used as a storage and distribution center. Every December, the entire space is used for the organization and distribution of some 200,000 Christmas gifts to needy children in the Dallas area. The gifts—toys, clothing, etc.—are all new, bought by individuals and companies who are matched with children's requests pinned on Christmas trees in malls or assigned to some 260 area companies participating in the program.

Army folks screen the families to confirm the children's eligibility. Then they create the trees—which are called "angel trees"—and make sure children are matched with angels, the gift donors.

Throughout December, some $3.5 million worth of presents stream into the warehouse, where they're checked in, verified with the children's requests, and placed in individual bags with the children's names on them. The shelves are three tiers high and run the length of a football field. And by distribution time, they're stacked high with gift bags.

The rush period is a week or so before Christmas when families come in at appointed times to pick up their children's gift bags. Think of that logistical challenge: 200,000 individual units catalogued and stored and distributed in less than a month, with most of the distribution crammed into a six-day period in which families are checked in and given the gift bags. In that period, the Dallas Army people greet and give presents to 180 families each hour. A pretty good warehouse operation by any standards, right?

Now, consider this: The Dallas Army people manage this annual program with just one full-time staffer assigned year-round. In December, that manager gets help from 40 or so employees drawn from other Army assignments or hired as seasonal workers. But the real manpower comes from volunteers, 100 per day, who come to the Army as individuals or from many of the same companies who are partners in the program.

Although many of those volunteers return year after year, on any one day most of the 100 could be first-timers who have to be assigned, trained, and supervised by limited staff. It could be chaos. But it isn't. The experience is so rewarding for many of the volunteers that Dallas organizers have waiting lists for some time slots.

Widen the focus just a little bit more: That entire December warehouse operation is *in addition* to all the other "businesses" The Salvation Army is involved in within the Greater Dallas area. Except for that one person assigned year-round to the project, the full-time Army staff is borrowed from programs that continue operating every day.

In 1999, in the Army's Carr P. Collins Social Service Center in Dallas, officers, employees, and volunteers provided emergency family assistance to 76,107 people, served 515,000 meals, helped 164,783 people find lodging, and supervised 453 children in day care. In the metro area's adult rehab centers, the Army worked with 2,185 men trying to overcome addictions to drugs and alcohol. Local Salvationists helped 9,629 disaster victims, assisted 12,347 prisoners and their families, located 94 missing persons, and sent 1,015 kids to camp.

In this one Texas city, The Salvation Army is a $23 million-a-year enterprise, with all the usual concerns about personnel, building maintenance, transportation issues, and financial management that level of revenue implies. And here's the evidence that our officers and employees pay careful attention to good business practices: Of that $23 million, only $1.6 million—*seven percent*—goes to the overhead expenses of administration, management, and fund-raising.

That's an overview and an introduction to our intentions for the coming pages. In the next eight chapters, we offer the essential elements of our approach. They aren't "the eight habits of successful spiritual enterprises" or "the eight-fold path to organizational happiness." They aren't even eight equally weighted principles. They are really one Big Idea and seven interconnected principles that flow naturally from it.

The Big Idea is *Engage the Spirit*. It has to do with that timeless question about "profit" posed by Jesus: "For what shall it profit a man, if he shall gain the whole world and lose his own soul?" (Mark 8:36, KJV) What you do and how you do it must be animated by a purpose that transcends quarterly earnings reports and that shines through your people and your programs.

The seven sub-categories are bottom-line principles connected with the Big Idea:

- **Put people in your purpose.** If you cannot convincingly explain how what you do serves human needs, you are courting failure in life and business.
- **Embody the brand.** By declaring accountability, by going public with your willingness to be tested against agreed-upon standards, you bolster your credibility, inspire your employees, and expand your potential market.
- **Lead by listening.** Without feedback—feedback that is sincerely encouraged and convincingly acted upon—an organization is blinding itself to what it needs to survive the forces of change.
- **Spread the responsibility, share the profits.** When you invest real power and real responsibility in your best peo-

ple and support them with your best methods, everyone has emotional equity in getting results.

- **Organize to improvise.** Not only should you accept the inevitability of change, you should be attentive to the ways it forces adaptations and rewards innovation.

- **Act with audacity.** People and organizations can grow only by taking risks—calculated risks, yes, but risks that nonetheless carry with them the risk of failure and the opportunity to learn from failure.

- **Make joy count.** Since the evidence is overwhelming that people work harder, longer, and more creatively if they are motivated by the intrinsic pleasure of their work, managers must do everything they can to make the value of jobs obvious and the joy in them accessible.

We'll draw heavily from specific examples in Army history and contemporary programs. But we'll also bring in examples from the corporate world to show how leaders of successful enterprises, including those with no relationship with The Salvation Army, operate with many of the same values.

We intend for you to take away practical suggestions, ways to apply some of our approaches. But since so much of our advice has to do with grounding organizations in a broader, more principled perspective, its real value is inspirational support. We really do want to talk about the meaning of life.

What we all need is to be reminded that certain transcendent values still—and will forever—apply in the real world and that we can't be happy or effective or close to who we really want to be unless we're integrating them into everything we do. We need to be encouraged—by example as much as anything—to act on what we know to be right and to have faith in what we know to be true.

We'll consider this book a success if it's nothing more than an antidote to cynicism. Cynicism is a paralyzing distraction and destructive to the spirit. Its operating delusion is that it's an appropriate response to evidence in the real world.

You can hear this voice of cynicism in every failed enterprise. Sure, it says, it would be a better world if people acted with compassion toward one another, if everyone told the truth, if spiritual values rather than material ones directed our strivings. But that's not the way the world works. To survive, to succeed, you have to look out for number one. You have to hoard your assets, lower your expectations, trust no one.

Our success, our record of growth over more than a century, offering the same "product" to an expanding global "market," is the countervailing argument.

As individuals, Salvationists are as unremarkable as any other man or woman you pass on the street. Not smarter, not stronger, not possessed of greater resources. Two things distinguish us, and both are available to anyone: An openness to God's grace and a commitment to demonstrating it through service to others.

Hoard our assets? We exhaust them in the effort to reach more and more people.

Lower our expectations? We are out to save the world.

Trust no one? Our best customers—and future partners— are drug addicts, prisoners, the enfeebled, and the desperately poor.

If we are naïve in our commitment, then God has blessed us for it, even if we count only the lesser blessings a hard-line business manager would acknowledge. We have survived and thrived for longer than just about any company in America. We are called "the most effective organization in the U.S." by the best-known management theorist in the world. By any material measure, our workers are vastly under-compensated; yet not only do we attract and retain dedicated life-long employees, we also have 3.3 million volunteers, many of them prominent in their communities and in the nation, who are eager to donate resources and time we could never afford to acquire or hire. And every year we are privileged to serve 30 million people, many of whose lives are transformed before our eyes.

Our world, we believe, *is* the real world. It's as full of hope as it is of hurt. All we have to do is open our eyes and let its reality liberate our hearts.

2

ENGAGE THE SPIRIT

How would people in your organization react to this job posting?

We're looking for individuals and couples to undergo two years of intensive training at their own expense, wear a uniform their whole career, subsist on a fraction of what they might be paid elsewhere, and spend most of their time with the homeless, the drug addicted, and other desperate people.

Successful candidates can expect to work long hours, often in inhospitable environments and, from time to time, in dangerous ones.

The job combines the responsibilities of a country parson and a city social worker. Medical skills are always a plus. So is accounting. And it's important that applicants be able to: drive trucks, put on puppet shows, play the cornet, coach basketball, sing harmony, negotiate real estate deals, cook for hundreds, and solicit funds on city streets and in corporate board rooms.

Are the lines forming yet?

As strange as it may seem, The Salvation Army attracts many people with many of those qualifications. In our classes of cadets at the four territorial officer training schools, we have kids right out of high school, and we have people who leave lucrative professions at mid-career. The percentage of cadets who are over 30, in fact, is increasing, which tells us two things: that The Salvation Army's mission resonates with many across the usual age boundaries—just as it does across gender, race, and ethnic classifications; and that at least some of the opportunities we offer transcend those available to even highly trained and experienced people who value our particular "compensation package."

Take Dorothy McBride, for example. Both her parents are Salvation Army officers, now retired. Initially, Dorothy invested her energies for service in higher education and the military, earning an M.B.A. and a Ph.D. in business administration while on active duty with the U.S. Air Force. In 1991, she was a lieutenant colonel with 21 years of Air Force service when she decided, at age 42, to become a Salvation Army officer. She attended her Air Force retirement ceremony on the Friday before Labor Day in 1991 and was starting up the ranks again in a different uniform, as a cadet in the Eastern Territory's School for Officer Training in Suffern, N.Y., on the following Wednesday.

As we write this, the former Air Force lieutenant colonel is a Salvation Army captain and director of curriculum at the training school. The change of uniforms was natural, she says. "It's just service in a different direction. In the military, you have the opportunity of serving the country as a whole. I wanted more of the feeling of serving others directly. And in The Salvation Army, that kind of outreach satisfies both a religious purpose and the purpose of meeting human needs."

Cindy-Lou Drummond and her friend, Martha Jenson, are making switches for similar reasons. Both women are physicians in their 40s. And both have been active as lay people with The Salvation Army in Lancaster, Pennsylvania, working with patients afflicted with AIDS and other serious conditions. In 1995, the two took three weeks from their jobs to work on a medical mission to Zambia.

No one would consider these two doctors lacking in spiritual passion or in selflessness. Yet both decided they wanted to get even closer to the core of Salvation Army work and become officers. So Drs. Drummond and Jenson will enter one of our two-year officer training schools, trading comfortable lifestyles and established practices for subsistence salaries and the frontlines challenges of Salvation Army work. Like Capt. McBride, these physicians see the transition as natural and full of opportunity.

"I'm just enhancing what I already have as a skill," says Dr. Drummond. "I'm hoping that blending medicine and the ministry of The Salvation Army will not only help people get well, but bring them to a saving knowledge of Jesus Christ."

What focuses our officers and employees and what attracts our volunteers has nothing to do with loyalty to a boss or commitment to a quarterly sales goal. You can't get that kind of dedication by merely promising fat bonuses or stock options. They have to get something else out of it, a payoff in some other currency. Even if you're not ready to put a name on it, you have to admit—given the scope and diversity of our work—it must be pretty powerful stuff.

In the vocabulary of our business, Salvationists are "called" to service. The call comes from God, through Jesus Christ, His son. And the model of service is Christ's example of compassion and undiscriminating love. Christ healed the sick, comforted the distressed, and extended forgiveness to those who stumbled. Almost always, He met the poor and the hurting where they lived and worked, instead of where it was convenient to receive them.

At the Last Supper, Jesus washed the feet of His disciples, symbolizing the attitude of service He expected from Christians: "For I have given you an example, that ye should do as I have done to you." (John 13:15, KJV)

And the scriptures are explicit about our responsibilities to one another: We are to feed the hungry, give drink to the thirsty, clothe the naked, and visit the sick and imprisoned as if we were attending the needs of Jesus Himself: "Inasmuch as ye have done it unto one of the least of these my brethren, ye have done it unto me." (Matthew 25:40, KJV)

This obligation is not a burden to bear. Rather, it's an opportunity to realize our best selves, to become who we were meant to be. Service helps activate the connection we all have with the divine.

The potential for this connection is embedded in our nature, put there by God. And we ignore it at our peril, not only as individuals, but as members of communities and as participants in organizations.

When people refuse to recognize their spiritual connection, they become disengaged from the larger purpose in their lives. They're easily distracted by temporary pleasures and traumas, by what's right in front of them minute to minute. Yet they feel disoriented. If you ask them what's troubling them, many will talk about how difficult it is to "balance" competing priorities in their lives—their careers; their families and relationships; their physical, emotional, and spiritual health. But balance isn't the issue.

Balance implies a static offsetting of forces. Children on a teeter-totter play at balance. They succeed when movement is arrested, when they are suspended, perfectly counter-weighted. But that's not something we can hope for in real-life problem solving. We can't suspend things in space or time. We can't stop change. What we need is to connect with something that accommodates change, that, in fact, *transcends* it. We don't need to balance the fragments, to juggle all the separate people we imagine ourselves to be. We need to integrate them into a whole, moving in harmony with a transcendent, divinely connected purpose.

One of the most straightforward descriptions I've heard of the way this process works came from a graduate of one of our rehabilitation programs. She had tried again and again to overcome her addictions, she told me. She had bounced from one treatment center to another. When I asked her how her experience with us was different, what finally got her on the path to recovery, this is what she said: "I went through all kinds of programs. But yours is the only program that went through me."

That's the validation we like. It celebrates an approach to living and working that moves *through* hurting people as if it were an axis around which they can organize themselves. We build our programs with that in mind. Our success rates depend on intensive, holistic strategies that treat our clients' immediate needs as interconnected and that assumes those needs are symptoms of a larger spiritual crisis in their lives.

A homeless addict, for instance, requires not only help in overcoming her addiction. She needs immediate housing. And she needs assistance in coming up with a long-range plan for a place to live once she's clean.

She's homeless because she doesn't have any money. And she doesn't have money because she has no job and, more than likely, little experience in managing what money she's made in the past. Even when she's free of drugs, she may have trouble finding a job with a future without job training. She can't get to employment interviews or to the work place without transportation. And without suitable clothes, she'll be uncomfortable in interviews and on the job. Recognizing all those needs puts us in the housing, job training, life-skills counseling, transportation, and clothing businesses.

What about her family? Perhaps she's a single parent with children she can't leave unattended while she works. And maybe her longtime addictions have inhibited her development as a parent and housekeeper. She might not know how to prepare healthy food for her family or to assume the most basic responsibilities of nurturing her children's intellectual, emotional, and spiritual growth. Understanding those dilemmas requires us to get into daycare, after-school recreation, healthcare counseling, and parenting instruction.

Each of those hurdles before a recovering addict can be an insurmountable barrier. Each is an invitation to fail, to despair at that failure, and then to escape to drugs. We can all agree that such a person's addiction makes it tough for her to make progress on any of these other fronts. But if she isn't helped to see there's hope in her situation, that it's possible to build a new life for herself and her family, how are you going to keep her off drugs?

So the task really is about more than just treating a chemical dependency or providing housing for the homeless or feeding the hungry. It's about salvaging and nourishing hope. Hope is the antidote for cynicism and despair. And you don't have to be homeless or addicted to drugs to know you need something to combat that poison.

Just about every problem with which we struggle festers in an atmosphere where nothing seems to matter, where lives seem purposeless and where the ability to influence change seems so limited as to be meaningless. People feel trapped, manipulated by powers beyond their—beyond anyone's—control.

This is a spiritual crisis. And it requires spiritual solutions.

People may have all sorts of physical hurts and needs, but their deepest wounds are related to the separation they feel from a sense of meaningful purpose. Many have come to believe that their lives cannot change, that the forces arrayed against them are too powerful. There may be some community of support and spiritual connection out there somewhere for others, but not, they believe, for them. They see themselves as unqualified, ineligible for grace. They are lost.

Finding themselves requires a personal commitment with profound social implications. Each individual must change—with God's help, we believe—from the inside out. They must leave the comfort zone of cynicism and *accept*—and that's the critical verb in the vocabulary of salvation, because it is freely offered—what has been true all along, that they are connected to a God that awaits their acknowledgment to reawaken His Spirit within them.

From the beginning, The Salvation Army was willing to run counter to the current of conventional wisdom of most organizations, including other religious organizations. We have always brought a message of inclusion and compassion to people used to being excluded and judged. We take seriously the commitment to service "without discrimination." No person—regardless of color, gender, nationality, religious faith or lack of religious faith, sexual preference, political ideology, or struggles with addiction or crime—is unwelcome. Even today, that's a radical notion of religious practice for some people. In England in the mid-nineteenth century, it was all but inconceivable.

William Booth, the Army's founder, was a Methodist evangelist who came of age during the social and economic turmoil of mid-nineteenth-century England. The Industrial Revolution had not only created great wealth for factory owners and investors, it had also been the principal catalyst for one of the great displacements of people in world history. Attracted by the wages of factories and mills, workers fled farms and villages for towns and cities. Most owned little more than the clothes on their backs; few had anything resembling a formal education. And when their ambitions proved greater than their opportunities, many overwhelmed sections of cities that became slums notorious for disease and dissipation.

The established religious denominations of the time, which depended primarily upon the loyalty and support of the middle and upper classes, were repelled by the squalor of those, in Booth's words, "who struggle and sink in the open-mouthed abyss." While some of those churches might open their doors to the poor if they cleaned themselves up and behaved like the gentry, most were unwilling to seek out the desperate and needy where they lived.

The Salvation Army, which began in 1865, was one of several offshoots of traditional denominations inspired to go where the established churches didn't dare. Booth and his wife, Catherine, despite having to struggle to support a family that would grow to include eight children, were passionate in developing their view of Christian purpose. That view, refined by the Booths' experiences with East End's desperate lot, entwined traditional Christian faith with a devotion to serving hurting people in what Booth identified as "the submerged tenth" of England's population. To Booth—and to all Salvationists to follow—the two missions are one. This is how he later explained it at an Army International Social Council in 1911:

"Our social operations are the natural outcome of Salvationism, or, I might say, of Christianity as instituted, described, proclaimed, and exemplified in the life, teaching, and sacrifice of Jesus Christ. Social work, in the spirit and practice which it has assumed with us, has harmonized with my own personal idea of true religion from the hour I promised obedience to the commands of God." Booth's "personal idea of true religion"—later capsulated in the slogan "soup, soap, and salvation"—took heat from both religious and secular critics. Church people were nervous about what they saw as unseemliness and sensationalism: the marching bands, the popular songs rewritten with religious lyrics, the open-air preaching, the impromptu prayer meetings in saloons and bawdy houses. And secular leaders were embarrassed by Booth's relentless exposure of the desperate conditions in which his "parishioners" lived, exposure which inevitably put pressure on officials to do something.

For defenders of the status quo, Booth's faith-based arguments for a social conscience ran counter to the "scientific" rationalizations for ignoring the less fortunate. The Army's campaign in the London slums came a half-dozen years after the publication of Charles Darwin's *Origin of Species,* which, upper-class social theorists believed, supplied a natural law to justify their indifference. They called it Social Darwinism. Wasn't the plight of the poor just another example of nature working its way with those who were less fit to survive? To interfere with nature's grand plan, therefore, would threaten the evolution of the species.

Booth had another vision of the grand plan. And for the most part, he and others with this broader view prevailed. Historians have often referred to this period as one heavily influenced by "the Social Gospel" and "muscular Christianity," when believers were challenged to apply their faith in God's saving grace not only in secure pews of comfortable churches but also on street corners and in desperate hovels where the poor and hurting were to be found. And what followed—especially in America—was a half-century of progressive movements and reform aimed at balancing civic responsibility and individual opportunity.

The theology of Salvationists today would be familiar to most mainstream Christians. We still closely resemble the Methodists, from whom William and Catherine Booth received their early religious education. And we share with Quakers, who lent the Booths space for some of the Army's first public meetings, a preference for simple and spontaneous observances of faith.

Early Army services have been described as "user-friendly: all were welcome, there were no reserved pews and no one gave worshipers disapproving looks if they were not dressed in their Sunday best."

User-friendly still has a nice ring. Our officers sign a life covenant with the Army proclaiming their commitment to Christian beliefs and principles. They and other members of the Army family will enthusiastically engage people who are interested in our religious doctrines. If you're involved in one of our rehabilitation programs, you'll be asked to take part in spiritual counseling. But we don't grab people by the lapels and preach them into submission.

Religious faith is not a prerequisite for admission to any of our social service programs. It's not required for most posts in the non-uniformed Army. And it's certainly not a litmus test for volunteers or donors, many of whom come to us from outside the Christian faith or without any specific religious orientation. Where we have rehabilitation or prison counseling contracts with government agencies, we can usually negotiate concerns about "proselytizing," provided guidelines don't require us to deny who we are.

Without our spiritual purpose, we would be just another organization with social service ambitions. Yet without our determination to meet human needs wherever they're discovered, we might just be another mainstream Christian denomination. What provides the glue for all the diverse elements in our approach is our belief that the most convincing argument we can make for a relationship with God is straight from the text of Jesus's example. We care for the hurting without discrimination and seek to awaken in them the same commitment and spirit of caring.

Remember what the former White House advisor, Bill Rhatican, said in the last chapter? He saw the "serenity and inner peace" the other clients derived from the spiritual focus of their recovery, and he wanted the same thing. Who wouldn't count inner peace as one of life's ambitions? Yet how many businesses organize themselves to make it possible?

The Salvation Army invests its money and its people's talents in all sorts of programs, from managing group housing and food service operations to providing job training and running retail outlets. But our core business is facilitating change in line with timeless values. If those values really are timeless and universal, they apply to everyone, regardless of where they work or how they count their profits. They transcend the goals of individuals and the strategies of organizations. How far, then, can any one person or any single organization get without acknowledging those deeper values and aligning their efforts with them?

Peter Drucker has noted the frustration of many junior executives in for-profit companies at the lack of opportunities to be engaged in work that taps deeper needs and rewards them in ways that have nothing to do with money or status. These students in Drucker's executive training programs come to him from everywhere in the business sector—from banks and insurance firms, from giant retail operations, from manufacturers, from new technology ventures. They're being groomed for top posts in their firms, which hand pick them for Drucker's programs. Most of these fast-tracked executives, Drucker found, also volunteer in nonprofits, devoting much of their limited free time to churches or the Girl Scouts or the local symphony.

"When I ask them why," says Drucker, "far too many give the same answer: Because in my job there isn't much challenge, not enough achievement, not enough responsibility; and there is no mission, only expediency."

Formulating an organizational mission without incorporating a commitment to the deeper, spiritual needs of human beings leaves you purposeless. You may be "bribed" (Drucker's term) by a high salary or an executive title. But instead of being meaningfully engaged in something important to you, you're stuck with manipulating processes, with moving around numbers on reports and names on organizational charts while you wait to be overwhelmed by forces of change.

If other organizations can find no other example to borrow from us, they should at least take this one: Not only do you not have to deny your spiritual impulse to get important work done in the real world, you will aid your every move by recognizing and embracing it. The spiritual connection is a constantly renewable source of energy. The Salvation Army runs on it. But think of the advantage of tapping into the same source for goals that may be slightly less ambitious than a commitment to save the world.

We in the Army are in a terrific position to see how spiritual need pushes people toward life-changing choices. The maturing of our cadet classes is one clear indication. So is the migration of professionals who come to us as employees and volunteers with skills we could never have otherwise acquired. Take, for instance, Carol Jaudes.

Carol Dilley Jaudes is an actress who has been a lay member of The Salvation Army since 1990. From 1994 until 1998, she performed in the New York cast of *Cats,* one of the longest-running Broadway shows in history. Since 1980, she had enjoyed a run of steady employment as an actor, a rarity in her profession. She was plugged into the New York theatrical scene and using that base for auditioning for her next move when a call came on Christmas Eve, 1998, from an officer she knew at Eastern Territorial Headquarters. Would she think about coming to work full-time with the Army to develop a theatrical ministry?

"Something like this had never occurred to me," she says. "But when I started talking to my friends in the theater about it, they understood instantly why I might want to do it. What's funny is that they understood even more than my friends who weren't in the business, who kept asking why in the world I would leave a Broadway show?

"The ten women I shared a dressing room with at the theater were my best friends. Only one out of the ten was a Christian. Yet they immediately understood why I might want to take my 18 years of training and experience, my passion for my craft, and use it to make a difference in people's lives."

Jaudes left *Cats* and began putting together a theatrical troupe for the Army. In the summer of 2001, she was planning her group's first conservatory to train actors from other Army units so they could go back and nurture a drama ministry in their towns.

"Not long after I left the show and started my new job," says Jaudes, "I went back to the theater to visit everybody. And before I left, one of the girls said, 'I am so happy for you. You're doing something that can help heal people.'

"Until then, I never thought of that word. But yes, there's the potential for healing in what I do now."

People such as Carol Jaudes's acting friends seem more likely than ever to identify with the need to invest talent and passion in service to others, perhaps because the contrast between what they need in their lives and what they're getting from most jobs has never been more obvious. Capt. Dorothy McBride, the former Air Force officer, says, "There's a fairly significant move right now among lots of people toward simplifying their lives, towards meeting your own needs at an adequate level and having enough left to reach out to others. There's a sense that too much materialism can drive you crazy. A simpler lifestyle serves your own spiritual and emotional well-being."

One reason we're noticing this attitude shift is the aging of the most trend-inspiring generation in American history, the baby boomers. They're entering the what's-it-all-about stage of life. And the partitions many in that generation erected between personal agendas and spiritual priorities are coming down. Here's another reason:

Over the last few years, wild swings in the so-called "new economy" driven by Internet-related businesses have created, if not a new set of spiritual believers, at least a whole new group of active seekers. Young entrepreneurs with the right product at the right moment made billions but were left thinking that something important was missing in their lives. Many others put everything in their lives on hold to build companies and careers that crashed when investors pulled the plug on the technology sector in 2000, producing all sorts of questions about the point of it all.

The fact is, at the beginning of the new millennium, there is more discussion about spiritual issues among people who consider themselves educated and sophisticated than at any time in recent memory.

Consider the growing acceptance of spiritual therapy in concert with medical treatment. Research suggests patients feel better, heal faster, and live longer when they identify strongly with religious traditions. Meditation and prayer are becoming more and more commonplace as aids to recovery from heart disease and chronic pain. And medical schools are now including courses in spirituality in their curricula.

Spiritually themed books such as *Conversations with God* and *Tuesdays with Morrie* are enjoying long runs on the bestseller lists. Magazines and newspapers that might have consigned such stories exclusively to religion sections a few years ago now seem interested in how people with religious perspectives apply them in social and business contexts. The fact is, American culture has been and continues to be a stew of spiritual seeking, and that inquisitive energy, we believe, is further evidence of the universal impulse for spiritual connection. Our role—and the role for other organizations eager to experience similar results and enjoy similar loyalties from customers and employees—is to provide an environment where the quest is respected and rewarded.

The spiritual perspective we advocate coincides almost exactly with the views of human nature that underlie modern principle-centered, people-oriented management theories. We believe God made humans to be caring, creative creatures. They learn, adapt, change, and help others to do the same. They, in fact, need to do those things to stay engaged with their surroundings and to feel fulfilled in their labors. And because humans are happiest when they are connected to a purpose beyond piling up cash or other material rewards, they're likely to choose challenging, fulfilling work for less money over boring, unfulfilling work with higher pay. This makes the job of managers very clear if organizations are to reach their highest levels of effectiveness: They must create and sustain environments that are challenging and fulfilling.

Since The Salvation Army can't afford to compensate people for jobs they're not interested in doing, our ability to get things done just about anywhere depends on leaders who understand how to build these kinds of working environments. Take, for instance, Irene De Anda Lewis, director of our Red Shield Youth and Community Center in the Pico Union section of Los Angeles.

The fifty-year-old center is in the heart of one of the poorest, most densely populated sections of the western United States. Most of the neighborhood residents are Latino and Korean immigrants, many of them struggling to stretch low incomes. Gangs threaten neighborhood safety. Street violence is common.

Yet over the ten years Lewis has been running the center, it's become a haven of safety, recreation, and education. More than 4,000 Pico Union kids and adults are members. There are programs going on nonstop through the day in the learning center, the indoor swimming pool, the gym, or the soccer field. Some 120 people participate in the Karate Club; 300 kids are in the Drama Academy getting professional instruction; and the facility—which takes up nearly a city block, with a new addition in the works—is headquarters for just about every neighborhood club and activity in the community. It has strong support from the police and the mayor's office and enough friends in the private sector and among nonprofit agencies and foundations that The Salvation Army has to contribute only about $117,000 of the center's annual $750,000 budget.

Lewis runs the place with 23 full-time staff people and 15 regular volunteers. She has nearly zero turnover in staff. Some have been at the center for more than 20 years. One of her volunteers, a teen who grew up with center programs before she moved to another part of the city, has to travel an hour one way to donate her time with the kids.

What explains this enthusiasm and loyalty from L.A. Red Shield's members and workers? It has to have something to do with Lewis's management style.

"When I came here," she says, "we had the standard organizational chart. You know, the one that has the executive director at the top, then the staff that reports to her, then the volunteers, and on the bottom all the people in the community.

"I said, 'Why don't we flip that around? Let's put the community on top, then the staff and volunteers, then me on the bottom. Let's see what the community wants. Then you tell me what you want me to do.'

"What my staff told me was that they could handle all the day-to-day operations of the center. They wanted me out in the community, listening and building relationships. So that's what I did. I went to the police department and the mayor's office. I went to clubs and foundations and neighborhood organizations. And out of that came all these programs the community wanted and all these partnerships with groups that help us."

Her role, says Lewis, "is not about micromanaging the center. It's about empowering the managers to let me do what I need to do."

Keeping all these programs running, continually expanding the center's community role—all of this is hard work, says Lewis. But the payoff for her and her staff is irreplaceable. "You get to see the change in the lives of these people," she says. "And that makes all the effort worthwhile. Without this center, these children would not have a safe place to grow up."

Contrast that approach to running an enterprise and rewarding workers with the one that comes out of "scientific management" traditions from the same industrial age that gave birth to The Salvation Army. Instead of integrating their lives' efforts with some transcendent purpose, workers were expected to merge themselves with machines. It didn't matter how disconnected they were from the results of their efforts, from the product that came off some distant end of a long production line. They were to focus entirely on the job in front of them. They were cogs in enormous wheels, parts of a machine fashioned and maintained by a manager class always on the lookout for faulty parts to fix or replace.

It's a view that, while softened in the post-industrial age, persists in every business sector. "Most companies are overmanaged and underled," write professors Gary Hamel and C.K. Prahalad. "It is fair to say that in most corporate headquarters, far more effort goes into the exercise of control than into the provision of direction." Just stroll through the warren of cubicles in any large company and note the number of "Dilbert" comic strips torn from newspapers and posted near workstations. The disconnection between managers and employees, the suspicion of motives, couldn't be more apparent.

Leaders with a spiritual perspective don't look at customers as demographic blips to be manipulated or employees as resources to be allocated. Since we're all connected by a common spiritual link, a human predisposition for acting in concert with a transcendent purpose, we are all partners in whatever enterprise we lend our energies to. Leaders have a responsibility to keep the view of that purpose uncluttered so it's visible to everyone at all times. It is that purpose, that overarching mission, that inspires confidence in customers and performance by workers.

In this way of looking at things, leaders don't waste their energies obsessing about control. They're working to free up possibilities, to tear down walls that block their people from developing innovative approaches to the mission. Like Irene Lewis, they are enablers.

When we begin working with even the most hurting beneficiaries, we don't let them get locked into a category of permanent service recipient. We want to help them move from dependence to independence, from helplessness to hope. And because we see them not only as customers, but as potential partners connected by common purpose, we're always looking for talents we can encourage and develop so they can become fuller participants in the community of caring.

We take this partnership idea literally. Many of the people in our residential rehabilitation centers begin working part-time with us as part of their recovery. Some become employees. Some are volunteers for life. Some even become officers.

In every program we have, we can point to those among us who sat right where the beneficiaries now sit. Some programs are run almost entirely by former beneficiaries. So there is no question that our high expectations for our new clients are justified. "Look," we say, "all of these people rebuilt their lives in this program. What can you say that they haven't heard—or lived? Doesn't their very presence validate our hopes for you?"

Because we expect so much, we make great demands. But the environment in which we make demands is exactly opposite the one you get with a cog-in-the-wheel perspective. If people see themselves as—and are managed as if they are—machine parts, every policy and procedure *they*, the managers, impose looks like an effort merely to tweak the gears and to suppress human creativity and individuality.

On the other hand, if you believe as we do that all humans want more than anything to connect with a higher purpose, it's logical to design the organization's approaches to facilitate that. When everybody buys into the purpose *we* are all working toward, then policies intended to streamline the design and speed its effects are seen as enabling, rather than limiting.

Our adult rehab centers are residence centers, and we prefer to have clients in residence for at least six months or so. Among the rules they must abide by are ones requiring total sobriety, attendance at individual and group counseling sessions, involvement in some kind of long-range plan for skills training or formal education, and faithful attention to assigned duties around the center.

All of these rules radically restrict the beneficiaries' options, especially given the street life many of them lived before coming to us. But each rule is necessary to maintaining the community and supporting the system that ultimately delivers freedom from dependence on drugs and alcohol. By agreeing to restrict and discipline themselves, residents get their lives back.

Salvation Army officers live by a lot of rules, too, rules that go far beyond their covenant of faith and their promise to live exemplary lives. They can't marry anyone who doesn't also agree to become an officer. They have to wear the uniform. They have to go where the Army tells them and live in quarters the Army supplies. But officers accept the restrictions as long as the policies are understood to be aids to focusing on what they joined up for, to save souls and to serve others.

The rules are not the point. The mission is the point. The rules only work when they're clearly in line with an overarching purpose visible from every perspective in the organization. Principles are what matter.

This view that an organization must create and refine its operations in accordance with some Big Idea seems counterintuitive to many business people. They think first of the product or service they intend to offer. Then they design processes to deliver it and policies to promote efficiency. They get greater productivity, they think, simply by putting pressure on the whole system to eliminate waste and increase output.

But if people are driven by an intrinsic need to connect with a purpose larger than themselves, then any system that doesn't provide that opportunity is asking for trouble. When you squeeze it for productivity without providing the incentive of purposefulness, people withhold their full commitment. They'll wait and see. They'll protect their own turf, drag their feet. And the whole operation can fragment and disintegrate.

Building an organization on core values that everyone understands and believes in, values that transcend the short-range goal of creating wealth for investors, is fundamental to the long-range success of any enterprise. We can say that as a religious organization that began with an idea and created a global structure to support and grow it for more than 135 years. Our faith in principle-driven management is an extension of our theology. But since these really are universal values we're talking about, you don't have to begin where we began to reach the same conclusion.

One of the most popular writer/consultants on personal and organizational change, Stephen R. Covey, argues for "the fundamental idea that there are *principles* that govern human effectiveness—natural laws in the human dimension that are just as real, just as unchanging and unarguably 'there' as laws such as gravity are in the physical dimension."

Thomas J. Peters and Robert H. Waterman, Jr., whose 1982 book *In Search of Excellence: Lessons from America's Best-Run*

Companies focused business leaders' attention on values-driven management, put it this way: "Every excellent company we studied is clear on what it stands for, and takes the process of value shaping seriously. In fact, we wonder whether it is possible to be an excellent company without clarity on values and without having the right sort of values."

In the preface to the paperback edition of *Built to Last: Successful Habits of Visionary Companies,* Jim Collins and Jerry Porras, explained why they thought their 1994 book became so popular: "We've met executives from all over the world who aspire to create something bigger and more lasting than themselves—an ongoing institution rooted in a set of timeless core values, that exists for a purpose beyond just making money, and that stands the test of time by virtue of the ability to continually renew itself from within."

If you're looking for an industry leader in the for-profit world who built a company with just those kinds of assumptions, consider Charles Brewer, the founder of the Internet service provider MindSpring. In 1993, Brewer, a Stanford M.B.A. tired of working in corporate environments he considered toxic, sat down and wrote up a nine-point set of core values and beliefs he thought should guide any company. He had no idea what business he was going to get involved in, what the product would be, even where he'd be located. But he made up his mind that the nine principles would be inviolate:

1. We respect the individual, and believe that individuals who are treated with respect and given responsibility respond by giving their best.
2. We require complete honesty and integrity in everything we do.
3. We make commitments with care, then live up to them. In all things, we do what we say we're going to do.

4. Work is an important part of life, and it should be fun. Being a good business person does not mean being stuffy and boring.
5. We are frugal. We guard and conserve the company's resources with at least the same vigilance that we would use to guard and conserve our own personal resources.
6. We insist on giving our best effort in everything we undertake. Furthermore, we see a huge difference between "good mistakes" (best effort, bad result) and "bad mistakes" (sloppiness or lack of effort).
7. Clarity in understanding our mission, our goals, and what we expect from each other is critical to our success.
8. We are believers in the Golden Rule. In all our dealings, we will strive to be friendly and courteous, as well as fair and compassionate.
9. We feel a sense of urgency on any matters related to our customers. We own problems and we are always responsive. We are customer driven.

When Brewer started MindSpring, he had the core values and beliefs printed on business cards and posted on its website, inviting employees and customers to hold him and MindSpring accountable. He hired people who bought into those beliefs and made strategic decisions based on them.

By the end of 1998, MindSpring had gone from 32 customers in Atlanta to more than half a million nationwide, from a work force of one—Charles Brewer—to 750 employees, from Brewer's initial $150,000 investment to annual revenues approaching $100 million.

MindSpring's reputation, built in the shadow of Internet giant AOL, was of a company true to its ideals. "The customers don't leave," said one stock analyst in 1998. "People stand in line to work there. [Brewer] created a corporate culture and then parlayed it into a company."

MindSpring merged with EarthLink in 2000, with the combined company, called EarthLink, becoming the No. 2 Internet service provider behind AOL. Brewer served as chairman for a short time, then cashed in his stock and began a search for another opportunity. Whatever would come next would be in the mold of his approach to building MindSpring.

"I wanted a company that would be different and better than the status quo," he explains. "The only place you can really focus is on the philosophy, the values inside, because everything else is so temporary. The people who are employed come and go. So the only thing that can be a permanent difference has got to be the philosophy."

3

PUT PEOPLE
IN YOUR PURPOSE

Kurt Weishaupt's life not only confirms Americans' cherished belief about the rewards of hard work, it also provides a dramatic illustration of the number one implication of our Big Idea: Part and parcel of our intrinsic need as humans to connect with something bigger than ourselves is our need to connect with and to help others.

Weishaupt arrived in this country in 1941 as a refugee of war with no money. Through his own entrepreneurial skill and perseverance and through—he would say—the timely aid of others, he built a fortune as a stamp trader and importer. Then he turned his attention to philanthropy, donating time and money to a number of charities, including The Salvation Army. He has spearheaded efforts through the Rotary organization's Gift of Life program and its subsidiary, Gift of Hope, which he founded, that have paid for operations for needy children around the world and provided many millions of dollars of medicines and aid to medical facilities in other countries. He also serves as a life member of our National Advisory Board.

Few could blame Weishaupt if lessons of compassion were not the most obvious ones he drew from in his own life. A German Jew, born in a farm village north of Frankfurt in 1913, Weishaupt was in his twenties when Hitler came to power. He and a friend were beaten by S.S. troopers outside a Frankfurt restaurant in 1935. So he moved to Italy, then to France, where, when the European war broke out in 1939, he was among a group of refugees imprisoned and slated for work duty in North Africa.

Weishaupt escaped from a prison train and, using forged papers, hid in French towns, waiting for a chance to reunite with his wife, then get to a port where they could get a ship to America. Befriended by a French priest, the couple was helped across the French border to Spain, where they were shielded by yet another acquaintance, who bought them safe passage to Portugal.

Although they could travel to America from Lisbon, they were stranded, because their American visas required them to have $4,000 they didn't possess. In a last-ditch effort, they turned for help to a Czechoslovakian they had met the year before in a Nice restaurant. Since that time, the Czechoslovakian had moved to Uruguay. Yet they were able to reach him, and, miraculously, based on that one restaurant encounter, he wired them the money.

There were so many moments, Weishaupt remembers, when it looked as if hope was lost. So many chance encounters that proved life changing. So many close calls. A traveling companion walking beside him in France was stopped by police, arrested, and shipped to Poland, where he was executed. Both of Weishaupt's parents died in concentration camps. Yet he and his wife survived to begin new lives in America.

"I believe," says Weishaupt, "that the many times our lives were saved have encouraged me in these later years, as soon as

I was able, to reciprocate for the wonders which happened—the incredible help we received, the many times our lives were saved from certain death—by the will of God."

What Weishaupt and millions of others endured in Western Europe just prior to and during WWII might be seen as one of the most compelling arguments for cynicism in the twentieth century. Yet what stuck with Weishaupt and transformed his life was not the evidence of man's potential for inhumane acts on a monstrous scale but the opposite—proof that even in the direst of situations, the need to help others not only perseveres, but can rise to heroic levels. That's what we mean when we say there are universal principles that remain true no matter where you come from or what you suffer, that these principles are connected to God's purpose, and that all humans are called to recognize that purpose and to integrate it into our lives. Kurt Weishaupt is living proof of the power of this spiritual impulse.

Weishaupt does not share our Christian faith, so he doesn't arrive at his commitment by the same theological route as Salvationists. He insists he's not even a religious man. Yet he not only feels moved to use his influence and his resources for the benefit of others, he feels grateful for the opportunity. Helping others, he says, has been "one of the most rewarding experiences of my eighty-plus years."

This is the place where our theory and our practice intersect. We believe that whatever purpose we and other organizations imagine for ourselves is meaningless unless it incorporates and inspires human aspirations. We believe God wants us to put people in our purpose. And we believe the admonition applies to all human activity, whether it's in church or corporate boardrooms.

Whether or not it states it explicitly, every organization sells itself as a service provider offering some product or process that promises to make people's lives easier, happier, or better prepared for adversity. Its results, regardless of the marketplace in which it operates, are entirely dependent upon the relationships—the sense of community—it promotes inside and outside its operations, which makes one of the key responsibilities of leaders the obligation to support processes that build and sustain a community of caring and eliminate those that inhibit it.

When William and Catherine Booth began their Christian Mission work in Victorian London, it was not as social revolutionaries or as founders of a new kind of church—and certainly not as new-era managers. They were evangelists who saw themselves as missionaries from established religion who would bring desperate souls into the fold, help them gain a foothold on the path toward a better life, then deliver them to churches that would continue nurturing their spiritual lives.

When that approach proved unworkable because of the reluctance of establishment churches to accept Booth's soldiers and because of the resistance of the soldiers to go where they weren't welcome, the Booths had just one alternative. They had to build a church—if not a literal one of spires and stained-glass windows, then at least a figurative one with a philosophy to match their mission of inclusiveness. And they had to do it right where they were, in East London, in the neighborhoods of despair. Given the context of the times and the Booths' passion, it couldn't help but be a radical enterprise.

During the Victorian Era, London was the world's largest city and a believable backdrop for Charles Dickens' popular fiction. It truly was the "best of times" and the "worst of times," with a soaring industrial economy and mounting evidence of a growing segment of the population left behind. East London in those days "was a city of its own," writes General Frederick Coutts, who held the Army's highest post from 1963 to 1969 and authored some seven books on its history and its principles of Christian service. The section was "separated from the

ʻtropolis by a wall of poverty so intimidating that
ınning by frontier guards."

ıllpox, and other diseases raged through sec-
ʍe ill-housed and the ill-nourished crowded
ʍr. Drunkenness, including drunkenness among young
children, was commonplace. And so was child abuse of every
sort. "It was enough to reduce any Christian soul to despair,"
says Coutts. Yet many Christian institutions turned away.

"[S]ave on Sundays," writes English journalist Richard
Collier, "few parsons had any faith in the common man; over
six thousand of them owed their livings to wealthy private
patrons. Some even warmly approved overcrowding—'it kept
the poor snug in cold weather.' " Booth, writes Collier, "had
nothing but his deep seated conviction to sustain him: the conviction that the church had failed the people."

Although the Booths' community-building efforts started
in the 1860s, widespread public awareness—international
awareness, in fact—probably began with the publication in
1890 of *In Darkest England and the Way Out*. An immediate
bestseller, the book appeared under Booth's name but was
probably ghost-written by W.T. Stead, a sympathetic news-
paper editor. There's little doubt, though, that it burned with
Booth's fire. It amounted to a declaration of independence, setting the Army's mission apart from both the established church
of Booth's era and from prevailing public opinion about the
causes of poverty. And it advocated an holistic approach long
before the word found its way into popular usage.

"I see the folly of hoping to accomplish anything abiding,
either in the circumstances or the morals of these hopeless
classes, except there be a change effected in the whole man as
well as his surroundings," wrote Booth and Stead. "To this,
everything I hoped to attempt will tend. In many cases, I shall
succeed, in some I shall fail; but even in failing of this my ultimate design I shall at least benefit the bodies, if not the souls

of men; and if I do not save the fathers, I shall make a better chance for the children."

To see how our experience in this purposeful integration points a way for all organizations, consider the effects the Booths' choices had, not only on the marriage of evangelical Christianity and social service, but also on the management model that evolved from committing to a transcendent purpose. Distancing the Army's work from both the support systems of the traditional church and secular society forced a series of decisions that made William Booth a manager, like it or not.

Once he fixed on the idea that social work "harmonized with my own personal idea of true religion," Booth had to build an organization beneath the movement. If he was committed to helping people who would not seek out a minister in the usual places, then he would have to locate his organization where the people were. And if he was going to establish such an organization independent of traditional sources of support, then he would have to develop a plan that reached out in at least two directions—to the needy who were the targets of his services and to potential foot soldiers and supporters who would provide the labor and the resources.

Although no one who's in a similar position considers it a plus, at least not while they're going through the experience, Booth had the advantage of choice-limiting poverty. There was no money for marketing studies. If the purpose he imagined for his Army was to have a chance to be realized in an actual organization, the relationships between strategies and results had to be pretty obvious. And nothing was more obvious than the necessity to look beyond old approaches to a new "market" and to new ways of raising money.

In Booth's time, established Victorian churches were focusing inward on bonds of class and convention that blocked their outward vision and ultimately left them on the sidelines for a social revolution they should have helped lead. They offered faith-reinforcing fellowship to their comfortable members, but the bridge to people in East London and beyond was left to Booth and the Army.

These days, leaders in most organizations know better than to argue—at least publicly—as some Victorian church leaders did, that they shouldn't be "distracted" from monitoring inside operations by the messiness of life outside their organizations. Focusing only on policies, processes, and relationships within a company is a fatal flaw. Ultimately, the effectiveness of any organization depends on the impact it has outside itself. In fact, the *only* reason the organization exists is to get results in the world beyond its walls.

It's easy to see how this fundamental reason for being becomes obscured. As a company culture matures, as its processes become more complex and its workforce larger and more diverse, managers become absorbed with strategies that are created more to satisfy internal needs for production quotas or quarterly earnings than to respond to the world outside. Fewer people inside the company meet their outside customers face to face. So they concentrate on the processes they believe to be successful, that *were* successful in the past—which works fine, as long as today and tomorrow are exactly like yesterday. Can you count on that in your line of work?

We can't do that in The Salvation Army. Our "market" of needy people shifts and evolves all the time. Neighborhoods become more diverse, forcing us to think about the best ways to reach people who speak different languages or who come to us from different cultural traditions. Suddenly, where there were mostly older people who required one kind of Salvation Army service, there are now immigrant families, many with small children, who require an entirely new set of approaches. Or the opposite may happen. Communities mature, increasing the demand for facilities and programs that address the concerns of an aging population. If we don't take notice of the ways in which our customers are changing and act on those changes, we'll become not only disengaged from the people we serve but from our mission as well. The two—people and purpose—are entwined. They cannot be separated.

Continuing to run a lean operation, even after success tempts you to build insulating layers into the decision-making process, helps you keep sight of what your purpose really is. But the sure way to avoid mission drift is to keep the focus on people both within and outside of the organization. Customers, employees, and investors will tell you what they need, what triggers their enthusiasm for your products and services, and what you have to do to earn and keep their trust.

Booth may be faulted as a product of his times when it comes to some elements of his management style, including a preference for autocratic decision-making. And we'll discuss that in later sections. But there's no doubt he happened upon an important approach with far-reaching implications when he committed to building the Army close to its prime "customers," from the front lines instead of from staff headquarters. Lack of resources may have made the decision easy. There wasn't money for much of a headquarters. But it didn't take long to see the advantages of locating operations within sight of the people who were the whole point of the enterprise.

One of the things he immediately learned, Booth told contemporaries, was that some of the old habits of his profession had to go. The sermonizing techniques he'd admired as a church evangelist, especially those that depended on flowery language or appeals to lofty theology, were of little use to him in East London. They just erected one more barrier between him and those he most wanted to reach. Far more effective were the lessons and appeals that came from the parishioners themselves.

Testimonies—first-person stories of transformation—rendered haltingly by men and women unaccustomed to addressing crowds quieted a rowdy meeting in seconds and anchored the message of salvation in the community of suffering. Communication was instantaneous.

Similarly, Booth found that one of the best ways to build outside support was to bring potential backers in direct contact with people the Army was serving. He welcomed visitors, including many of the well to do, to the kitchens and rough dormitories. He invited supporters and critics alike, and he cultivated friends in the press. Reducing the physical distance between beneficiaries and benefactors helped diminish the psychological barriers to community, making it easier for everyone to see their connections with one another and their opportunities to fulfill their need to serve. "My visitors say," said Booth, "that visiting is almost impossible without the means of relieving the people."

This idea of community is crucial to our "theology of service." Humans are linked in a family with God. We are truly brothers and sisters, equal in our eligibility for grace and transformation. When we heed the call to reconciliation in that family, we can see the links that connect us more clearly and can begin to honor and strengthen the bonds.

It makes no sense, then, to behave toward our beneficiaries as if we're merely performing charitable acts for a less fortunate class or, as managers, to behave toward colleagues as if we are more worthy and privileged. After all, these roles are something we assume only temporarily. And over the course of our lives, the roles may be reversed many times. Need moves back and forth along the lines that connect us like electrons in closed circuits. We are all, literally, in this together.

The failure to understand and support this sense of community costs organizations at every level. Peter Drucker connects the shortcoming to at least two reasons "business has, in many ways deteriorated badly in the last 20 years. One reason is the enormous discrepancy between those insane salaries at the top. When I look at the people in my executive management programs—45 year-olds, upper middle-management—they are not only alienated from their top management, they are contemptuous of it. They are resentful because of the greed at the top.

"Secondly, these [executive management students] feel that the senior people have no respect for honest work. [The senior managers] look upon that engineer or that chemist or that sales person as a peon.

"Organizations that don't see people as a resource but as people, as creatures created in the image of God, have a very different atmosphere. You don't have to call them 'spiritual,' because that has religious overtones, and these are not necessarily religious in that sense. But they see themselves as communities, not just as payrolls."

Of course, we don't have qualms about calling that sensibility spiritual or religious, since that's the base from which we operate. But the language is less important than the commitment. Operating from this perspective is what helps to give The Salvation Army our results-leveraging advantage and is what qualifies us as, in Peter Drucker's view, "venture capitalists." Everyone is a customer. Everyone is a potential partner.

Let's talk about a contemporary example of how the theory of community partnership works. We have a childcare center in the Dorchester section of Boston that serves some 40 parents in a neighborhood that is one of those urban battlegrounds where crime and illiteracy threaten the best efforts of citizens and organizations. The community has a long list of needs, more than we can possibly serve with our limited resources. Yet because we are committed to an holistic approach, we are determined to make an increasing difference in the lives of families there.

Here's one way we could tackle those problems: We could play the role of social service experts. After all, this is territory in which we have a lot of experience. We could bring in some specialists to decide the most pressing needs, get some grant money, then launch programs to attack what we identify as high-priority issues—perhaps with the help of outside consultants or government partners.

But if you're not careful with that kind of approach, you end up casting the people in the neighborhood as victims and yourself as rescuer. These roles have a way of solidifying, so that before you know it, you have made the relationships permanent. It's always your job to hand out charity; always their job to need it. Resentment and frustration build on both sides until the money runs out. Then, you're back where you started from, facing seemingly intractable dilemmas with even fewer resources and with even higher cynicism from customers and potential investors.

There's not enough money, not enough staff people and volunteers in the world to support a permanent population of rescuers and victims. Better to put the energy into a strategy that unlocks those roles, that stands a chance of multiplying the resources you bring to the problem by cutting through the cynicism and turning care recipients into care givers—which gets us to the approach of Salvation Army staffers in Dorchester.

In 2000, Army people began what Chris Hogan, who's in charge of Army social services in that area, calls "a community-based conversation." And they started with parents of the kids in the center, letting them know they'd like to speak with them individually about how they—the parents and neighborhood residents—viewed the challenges facing them.

They formed a team of experts who visit homes, but only at the invitation of parents. And the meetings really are conversations. "You end up with an action step," says Hogan. "But you don't go in with an agenda. For an hour and a half or so, we just talk about what they know about the community, about who they are as individuals and what they want for their families."

Issues arise without much prompting. For instance, some of the working parents with jobs that start before our center opens wanted earlier operating hours for the facility. There was no money for that, our people told the parents. But they didn't let the subject drop. They asked if maybe there was some other solution that didn't require raising more money or hiring more people. They threw it open for discussion: If we consider this together, they asked, if we think about what each of us can bring to the table, is there some way we can accommodate these parents' particular needs?

One of the other mothers volunteered a solution: She could babysit some of the kids until the child center opened if parents would bring them by her house on their way to work. Then, she'd take them to the center when she took her own kids.

Almost immediately, says Hogan, this woman took it upon herself to make that idea work. "She began to see herself as a leader. She didn't know she had it in her."

For the Army staffers and volunteers, says Hogan, "there was this sense of relief. You suddenly realize it's not all on you. You don't have to lead all the time. There was this incredible sense of energy. People in Dorchester started to say, 'We're going to take back this community house by house.' "

The big advantage in this approach is not just the ideas that come when people put their heads together. It's the change in attitude, the dropping away of cynical assumptions that "that's just the way things are" and the realization that individual efforts—even something as simple as babysitting another mother's children for an hour or so—have community impacts.

"You can measure hope when people are standing up and taking responsibility for their community," says Hogan.

What's happening in Dorchester and in other places where the Army is leveraging limited resources by treating customers as future partners are examples that can be applied in other organizations. In evangelical religion, of course, conversion has a precise meaning. It's all about transforming the lives of the lost, bringing them to salvation through God's grace. It's at the heart of what we do. And there is no substitute for this specific, sacred kind of transformation. Yet we think William Booth and the early Salvationists, who were so fond of eliminating boundaries between the sacred and the secular, would approve of using the concept of conversion in a broader metaphorical sense.

Already, businesses turn to the language of conversion to describe a process that's a kind of measure of productivity. In real estate, for instance, developers talk about converting those who've put a minimum deposit on some piece of property to customers who sign a contract. In magazine publishing, circulation managers talk about converting customers who may have been attracted by some promotional offer to regular subscribers. Most businesses, in fact, are about converting prospects to paying customers.

Now, take one more step back. Organizations are also trying to convert tentative employees to engaged loyalists, one-time supporters to continuing investors, first-time customers into regulars, and regulars into word-of-mouth advertising. Transformation is built into every business plan.

The Salvation Army could not survive—let alone grow its programs—without being effective at this broader conversion concept as well as its commitment to personal spiritual transformation. The 5,000 minister-officers at the core of our "company" are the engines of our enterprise. Yet, alone, they couldn't begin to manage our 9,000 centers, let alone the thousands of programs we provide on a 24-hour-a-day, seven-day-a-week, coast-to-coast basis.

At one point in the early stages of the Army in England, William Booth found it necessary to issue "General Orders Against Starvation" to prevent his staffers from using their own rations to feed others. Such is the demand in our "market," we'd have to do the same thing without our unpaid supporters, our 3.3 million volunteers, who are "converted" to service by their association with our officers and with one another. They are not just adjuncts to our organization. They are essential to our mission. And it is the multiplier effect of their combined efforts that accounts for our ultimate effectiveness.

Consider a couple of modern-day multipliers. To begin with, our famous thrift stores—1,600 of them nationwide—are models of the conversion technique. Discarded clothes, household items, even automobiles are converted to retail inventory for stores that primarily serve patrons who need the bargains we provide. The profits from the sales go to sustain the Army's Adult Rehabilitation Centers. And at some stage in their rehabilitation, clients of the centers are often assigned to the stores to learn basic business and people skills. Some, after they've completed their programs, become paid managers.

In Las Vegas, some of our entrepreneurial employees and clients created the Campus Corner Café, which has the potential for broadening the conversion effect even more. With all the hotels and restaurants in town, the demand for cooks and kitchen help is always high; so the local community college offers professional kitchen training courses, and the state of Nevada provides tuition money for students who qualify by need. Sue Markham, one of our employees in Las Vegas, figured out a way to link our people with the community college program and with state job-training funds. She gets our rehab clients into these 90-day kitchen training courses. If they complete the course, they're guaranteed jobs in Las Vegas restaurants.

While they're going to class for 15 hours a week at the community college, our program participants help us out in our homeless food service, which feeds anywhere from 1,000 to

2,000 people a day. And in 2000, with these extra chefs-in-training, our people opened a sit-down café, where anyone with a $2 token can be fed from a menu of favorites, such as hamburgers and hot dogs, plus daily specials. Waiters, also clients in our rehab and homeless programs, take the orders and deliver the meals to tables.

The $2 token is good only at the café. Street people can buy the tokens. And area residents and businesses purchase them in bulk, then give them away, as a way to make sure their support for the homeless goes directly to wholesome meals instead of to booze and drugs.

This is a classic Army approach. In fact, a token system very similar to this was used in an Army program in England more than a century ago. The principles—like the purpose—remain the same. Rehab clients, in the process of transforming lives that may have hit bottom, get a new direction and maybe a new career. They also get the satisfaction of applying their training immediately and of serving those as needy as they were before they became involved in our programs. Client becomes service provider.

In supporting the token program, business people and Salvation Army backers in Las Vegas get the satisfaction of helping the homeless in a way they know is effective. So some of their frustration at the seemingly hopeless problem is converted to a sense of possibility.

The Army's investment of resources in the transformation of clients is rewarded by what can easily become a self-sustaining, entrepreneurial enterprise run primarily by folks who were desperately in need just a few months before. Once the program is up and running, not only is there the potential dollar return on our investment, there is also the harder-to-measure value of the café as an example of hope. It represents a small but highly visible step back into the mainstream for many who thought they had been marginalized for life.

Programs like these wouldn't have occurred to us if we weren't in the habit of asking endless versions of this question: How can we help current beneficiaries, once they're on paths to reconciliation and recovery, take the next step toward helping others? And that question would never come up if we didn't believe in the potential of all people, no matter how alienated they may appear, to rejoin the human community and to contribute to it.

You don't have to run thrift stores or rehabilitation centers to gain the benefits of people-centered decision-making. There are lots of ways in which organizations get multiplier effects from innovations, everything from new products created from the waste materials it took to make old ones to money-saving shortcuts suggested by customers. Almost all of the stories about such innovations talk about the welcoming atmosphere in which those ideas were proposed and implemented. It's an environment in which people feel confident someone is going to take their bright ideas seriously.

Managers create that atmosphere by consistently demonstrating that people count more than processes, by cultivating a community of trust and support. And, as William Booth learned, the way to boost that sense of community is to let people feel it for themselves by direct contact—benefactors with beneficiaries, employees and managers with customers.

You'd think we have an advantage there, given all our social service programs. But remember the large and complicated operation we need to keep all those programs running. Just like every other big company, we need lots of behind-the-scenes people—computer programmers, transportation specialists, janitors, accountants—who might never have direct contact with our beneficiaries. So how do we get them to feel the power of the mission and of the community it implies?

We take great pains to do what any organization can do. We create opportunities for people on our staffs to tour social service facilities and rehab centers, to meet social workers and beneficiaries, to hear about programs, and to volunteer in them. They're welcome, also, to spend time with counselors or in prayer and meditation at our chapels. And we provide many of these opportunities on what would be considered company time. Our desk-bound senior officers are expected to spend part of every month in communities, not only meeting with managers who report to them, but also mingling with employees and lending a hand directly in programs. We call it "getting your heart warmed."

I remember a particular visit Alice and I made to Detroit in 1997 when I was national commander. We were there to take part in an Easter Sunday service at the Harbor Light Center. The Army's Harbor Light centers are often the first step off the streets for the homeless and addicted, so they're really the frontlines of our work. They're the places where our people are challenged and inspired in dramatic ways. And the one in Detroit was no exception, especially on Easter Sunday.

The service was on an upper floor of an older multistory building in Detroit. And it was jammed with people. They were singing and swaying with the gospel music. In fact, the whole place felt as if it were swaying. I remember wondering if the old place could stand that much enthusiasm. But no one else seemed to be worried, and the feeling of joy in the Lord's work was so infectious it swept just about everything else from my mind.

What was especially moving about that service were the testimonies, the stories of personal transformation experienced by people who came to this Harbor Light from all manner of sad struggles with alcohol, drugs, and the street life. One woman I'll never forget stood and told her story of being hopeless in her addictions, of dropping out of school and feeling her chances for accomplishing anything were over. Then, she produced an 8×10 envelope, and out of it she pulled her new high-school diploma, earned after she'd gotten herself clean and back on track with the help of Harbor Light and other Army programs.

Her testimony was warmly received. And she stood there glowing from the effects of the acknowledgment. This was a congregation that knew a thing or two about the temptations and doubts this woman had to overcome to stand among them and proclaim her faith. And you would have to be unconscious, insensible to human communication of any kind, to be in that room with these people and not be moved by their personal triumphs and renewed in conviction about the power of God's purpose in all our lives.

That's what I mean when I say it's important to "get your heart warmed," to put yourself in position to feel renewed by direct contact with your customers. Executives must make such opportunities high priorities. And it's not easy. In a large company, if you're not careful, you participate in the lives of employees and clients through networks of intermediaries. You insulate yourself from the sound of the music, from the joy and the drama of engagement between your organization's purpose and the people it serves.

Alice and I were invited to speak at that Detroit Easter service. And I'm sure we did. But I can't remember what I could have offered that room of believers and seekers that compared to what they gave me. Leaders who don't build that kind of opportunity into their schedules are forfeiting an advantage they need both for their own mission focus and for the decision-making processes throughout their organizations.

What does *people contact* have to do with organizational focus? Everything.

If we, as Salvation Army leaders, are confident we're in harmony with our spiritual mission, we can make just about every other decision by answering questions such as these: "What does this have to do with helping hurting people?" and "Is this the best use of our resources to help people we're pledged to serve?" If we can't define a policy or a proposal or even a long-standing program on those terms, it has to go.

Managers in other enterprises can generalize these test questions to this one: How is this decision going to affect the lives of our customers? That's it. If you can't demonstrate that what you propose is going to create value for people, it's probably the wrong choice.

For most organizations, it's easier to imagine the people-serving potential in new ideas than it is to pull the plug on old ones that are losing value to customers. Saying "no" or "no more" can be a painful exercise, especially in cases where an organization is heavily invested, both in terms of physical resources and in terms of identity. Here's a good example.

In the early 1990s, we owned a hospital complex in the New York City area that had grown from a small Manhattan facility for unwed mothers in the earlier parts of the century to an enormous medical center and teaching hospital in the Flushing section of Queens. The center was associated with nearly 1,000 doctors, and it had earned the respect of both medical professionals and regional residents. In terms of capital investment, it was the Army's largest single holding in America and even carried the name of The Salvation Army's founder. It was the Booth Memorial Medical Center.

But the center, one of the last Salvation Army general hospitals in this country, was an expensive enterprise, already accounting for one-quarter of the Eastern Territory's annual budget of more than $400 million. And that amount would have to increase if we wanted to maintain the level of services our doctors and patients had a right to expect. We would have to invest $100–150 million in upgrades, most of it borrowed, in an era in which we could expect sources of revenue from government and private insurers to diminish. At some point down the line, its mounting debts were likely to overwhelm the territory's resources.

We invited independent experts to help us evaluate every option. And the case for selling the hospital center while there was still a chance to find a buyer was overwhelming. Think of the soul-searching this generated within our organization. There were Salvation Army officers whose careers were wrapped up in the services Booth Memorial provided. There were medical professionals who were not Salvationists but who came to know and respect us through the operation of this hospital.

For many in the region, this complex represented us. It was a franchise we founded and nurtured to prominence. For a time, it was an important means toward our mission of saving souls and helping people. But if we allowed it to absorb more and more of our energy and money, it could dilute our effectiveness, ultimately depriving more people than we could serve with the hospital. We made the only decision we could in light of our responsibility. We sold Booth Memorial.

Now, in business terms, this could be seen as the forfeiture of a franchise. Given the pride we had in the history of the hospital and its connection to the Army, we could have dug in our heels and pledged our energies to raising the enormous sums the hospital needed. But we would really be borrowing those energies and that money from other Salvation Army efforts, which would, in turn, be in deficit. And we couldn't justify such a narrow, expensive commitment in the face of our overall mission.

It's easy to get caught up in the process of an enterprise, to keep on doing what you've always done, because you're good at it. But if you're always testing your approaches against your mission, the franchise you build has less to do with a specific program than it does with the purpose that's really at the center of your business. And ultimately you get credit from all your customers—the ones on the receiving end of your service, the ones doing the serving, and the ones investing their time and resources supporting you—for focusing on the point of all enterprises: people.

The adjustments you make to keep your processes aligned with people's needs don't have to be monumental. Small changes can begin a turnaround. Consider the situation Majors Bill and Victoria Edmonds found in the summer of 2000 when they took over the Harlem Temple Corps at 138th Street and Lenox Avenue in New York City. For years, our people had operated classic Salvation Army programs there, serving the needs of a maturing African-American population. But the neighborhood has changed into one of the most multicultural in New York. Major Victoria Edmonds estimates there are 17 distinct cultures represented from Central and South America, the Caribbean, and Africa.

One of the traditional programs at the corps was a Christmastime performance by a girls' tambourine ensemble. "And we decided to take on the challenge of doing something totally different than the way it had been done for 25 years," says Major Edmonds.

Instead of insisting that the girls adhere to standard music and performance styles, she encouraged the ensemble to reflect the heritages of the immigrant cultures. "It was Spanish music they played," says Major Edmonds, "and I told them to put a little dance to it. It wowed the people."

Such a simple alteration often carries symbolic weight. In the Edmonds' Harlem corps, people took notice that The Salvation Army took notice of them. Now, more and more people from the neighborhood are participating in expanding Army programs. The Edmonds have a daily lunch program that feeds 75 to 100 people. They have 80 kids in the center after school, and some come back for character-building classes at night. There are computer classes with 35 to 40 people, a new women's craft group, and exercise classes in the works.

"You actually see people catch a new vision," says Major Edmonds. "They can see the past doesn't have to determine the future. They're ready to try new things."

Of course, it often takes great patience to get the full benefits of people-centered strategies. When your purpose is tied to people, so are your processes, which means you are at the mercy of imperfect plans and inconsistent performance. You have to forgive mistakes and ask for forgiveness of the ones you make. But just as you can demand more from members of an organization when they buy into the overall mission, you escape the worst consequences of your blunders when everybody believes the missteps were made in good faith.

In an organization that provides a sense of community, foul-ups are aberrations that are easily addressed and corrected. They stand out as accidental deviations. But in an organization in which workers have reason to be cynical about mission clarity and managers' commitment, people come to suspect the "real" reasons behind every policy. Each management miscalculation confirms the paranoia. And operations can slow to a crawl.

If people are more worried about what's going on inside the operation—about the hidden agendas of bosses—than what's happening outside with customers, it's hard to convince them to take on new challenges. They're too consumed with protecting turf and undermining rivals. And a lot of time is wasted covering up potential problems and ducking responsibility.

That's why having a clear, principle-centered mission invested in human potential is not just an idealistic way to lead. It has immediate practical benefits, especially when it comes to energy management. Once you establish—and your people believe—that your purpose is integrated with the highest human aspirations, then the energy you don't have to use convincing them to trust each new initiative can be applied directly to helping them succeed and to making course corrections when they're needed.

In this sense, the leadership of the organization is indemnified. A bad manager here and there, a disappointing performance in one sector, even a tragedy that makes you question a key strategy—none of that inflicts irreparable damage, provided everyone buys into the ultimate purpose for their labors.

Even with all our experience at seeing the multiplier effect of serving others, we still miss opportunities. Our front-line officers and workers would roll their eyes if senior staffers bragged about how wondrously efficient we were in every program we undertake or in every personnel decision we make. We don't always make the right choice the first time around. But if we really are paying attention to the people part of our purpose, often we'll get chances to get it right in the long run. Take, for example, the story of Major G.

Romolo Giudice, a Chicago-area tough, began selling drugs when he was still in his teens. He was in and out of juvenile detention, then county jails, then the Illinois State Penitentiary. He remembers one judge looking at his long rap sheet and pronouncing him incorrigible: "There isn't any hope for you. You are an addict. You will never change."

But after one arrest, Giudice found himself in a Salvation Army adult rehabilitation center in lieu of more prison time. And for a change, he fell in with the right crowd. Reluctant at first, he gradually came to believe that he could turn his life around. He became as enthusiastic in his new Christian life as he was in his old one as a street hustler. And in 1964, when he married his wife, Georgann, at the Army rehab center, Giudice had set his heart on becoming an Army officer.

Uneducated except for street smarts, tattooed, aggressive in a style calculated to frighten many folks, Giudice—he'd have to admit himself—was probably not the obvious, ideal candidate for officership. He was turned down three times. Yet he persisted. Finally, he and his wife were accepted. And they were commissioned as officers in 1966.

Over the course of the next 32 years, the Giudices served in posts in the Central and Western territories. Rising to major—Major G, he came to be called—Giudice never lost his rough edges, but that turned out to be an advantage. He was especially good in the adult rehabilitation centers and with social work. Who could tell him something he had not heard—or done?

We salvaged the multiplier effect, in this case, because two important things were happening more or less at the same time. First of all, Giudice believed so wholeheartedly in the community The Salvation Army represents, he was determined, no matter what, to join the officer group that is at its core. Our institutional reputation—our brand (and we will talk more about this in the next section)—can enjoy that kind of appeal only when we're able to consistently demonstrate that we are who we say we are. So it was a good sign Giudice wanted to become an officer even when we weren't sure we wanted that—which gets us to the second good thing we had working for us.

Because part of the proof of who we are is how we act on our promise to honor human potential over human failings, we were compelled to take a second look—or, in this case, a fourth look—at Giudice's officer candidacy. Even though both he and Army decision-makers took a while to get on track, Giudice, the Army, and all whom he touched in those three decades were ultimate beneficiaries. We all survived our mistakes. There was forgiveness all around.

When he retired in 2000, people Major G had helped over his career came from Nebraska, Illinois, Hawaii, and California to help him celebrate the transition. And even in retirement, he went back to work for the Army. At this writing, he and his wife are in Las Vegas, where Major G oversees the thrift stores—

another of his specialties, partly because of the merchandising and sales skills acquired during his street-hustling days.

Of all the advice to business managers through the years, "putting people first" is probably the most often repeated—and the most often neglected. Still, we in The Salvation Army couldn't be more adamant about it. We say you can't have an effective organization without a commitment to a purpose that transcends the mere material. And we say you can't have a purpose that doesn't have a concern for people at its core.

Where we may differ from others who've offered the same admonition is in our authority. Nothing could be more clear than our mission. We are here to save souls and serve others. Concern for people—their salvation, their physical and mental health, their potential for freeing themselves from cynicism to help others—drives everything we do. The fact that that is our *only* business and that we have thrived and expanded our operations for more than a century in America undercuts arguments that organizations can't afford to put people first.

But what if your business doesn't offer the same kind of intrinsic rewards we get from our efforts in The Salvation Army? What if it requires workers to be dutiful and efficient but doesn't afford much of a chance for them to experience customers' satisfaction? How do you get the advantage of putting people in your purpose under those conditions?

One of our favorite examples of inspirational management in an unlikely business sector is Bob Byers, who is chairman of a family company, Byers' Choice in Chalfont, Pennsylvania. The company grew from a hobby of Joyce Byers, Bob's wife, who handcrafted Christmas figurines—carolers dressed in Victorian-era costumes—for friends at the holidays.

When the figurines became so popular that Joyce and the rest of the family couldn't keep up with the demand working out of their living room, they hired an employee and moved operations into the garage. That was in 1978.

By the end of 2000, Byers' Choice had produced hundreds of thousands of the figurines, still handmade but now with the help of 180 employees in a manufacturing facility on 26 acres of land outside of Philadelphia. Bob Byers estimates that, at $21 million in annual wholesale sales to some 3,000 retail outlets in the United States alone, Byers' Choice is the largest producer of handcrafted figurines in America.

Making these figurines is tough work, especially on the hands. And the effort to produce them at a profit requires factory-like methods. It's difficult, repetitive work of the kind that many manufacturers have taken overseas where wages and worker expectations are lower. But Byers' Choice turns a comfortable profit with a loyal workforce. "Our accountants once told us," says Byers, "that we were one of the most profitable companies they'd seen."

The work at Byers' Choice is physically demanding enough that Byers expects that, over time, most of his workers will have to rotate out of line work or leave the company altogether. He plans for that, offering to help them find jobs elsewhere when they can no longer comfortably work in figurine assembly. Even he is surprised, he says, when so many of his former employees stay in touch and continue to pass the word about what a good organization Byers' Choice is long after they've left the payroll.

What's his secret? If he can't offer the pure pleasure of labor, Byers figures he can at least provide a context in which it's clear what the priorities are. It's God first, he says, then people—customers, employees, and community. And he demonstrates the people commitment with company resources.

Besides the usual premium benefits you'd expect from a company that wanted to be known for its attention to employees—benefits such as a pension plan that requires no worker contribution—Byers' Choice provides extras, such as a $2,500 college scholarship for each child in a worker's family. It adopts a needy child in a Third World country in the name of each employee and encourages workers to keep up correspondence with the kids. And as a measure of its commitment to the wider community, the company donates 20 percent of its profits every year to some 350 charities and nonprofit organizations.

"Initially, I was hesitant to make public how much we were giving away," says Byers. It sounded too much like bragging. But he became convinced, he says, "that each community needs role models for others as individuals and as companies."

He was also worried how his employees might take the news that money that might have gone to increased salaries and bonuses was going to charity. "I was absolutely elated," says Byers, "to find that they were very, very proud to be working for an organization that does so much for other people."

What better argument for the bottom-line value of a focus on people? "I can't explain it," says Byers. "There's just an enormous amount of pride in working here, in working for an organization that does things right."

4

EMBODY THE BRAND

In 1997, Joan Kroc, the widow of the founder of McDonald's and a well-known philanthropist in her own right, was driving through East San Diego with former Mayor Maureen O'Connor. San Diego's metro region is one of the most beautiful and one of the most affluent in America, yet there are people there just as desperate and needy as our clients in any other location. In East San Diego, citizens seem especially cut off from the safety and prosperity of neighborhoods just a few freeway exits away. Families struggle to get by. Children with too few options after school drift toward trouble, including the criminal trouble of gang activity.

Concerned about what might be happening to these families, the two women talked about possible ways to create opportunities, especially for the kids there. The key question: If the right resources were available, what agency or organization could make the biggest difference in those neighborhoods?

The Salvation Army, came the answer.

Now, we're proud of our San Diego network of support, which—by the end of 1998—was helping us maintain a $37-million annual budget in the division and deliver services to almost a quarter million people. But the former San Diego mayor was not part of that formal Army network. She just knew about us from her time in city government and from working with community organizations.

Nor was Mrs. Kroc among our major donors. So our people were surprised by her call and the invitation to come up with ideas for some kind of project in the community she and Maureen O'Connor had driven through.

Not knowing exactly what Mrs. Kroc had in mind, Art Stillwell, who heads our development efforts in the San Diego area, drafted several alternatives escalating in scope and cost. She sat through the presentation of options and said, "I like it."

"Which part?" Stillwell asked.

"The whole thing," she said.

The whole thing turned out to be a $94 million project, with Joan Kroc contributing $87 million to build and maintain it. The Ray & Joan Kroc Community Center, encompassing five major buildings on a 12.5-acre site, will become the largest Salvation Army community center in the world. There will be an ice skating rink, an aquatic center, a climbing wall, and all the usual recreation facilities for basketball and other sports. And there's a 600-seat performing arts theater, with practice rooms and studios.

When the announcement came in 1998, it was front-page news throughout the country. Eighty million dollars. The largest single pledge in Salvation Army history.

So here's the big question: Why us? With her resources and network of connections, Joan Kroc could have hired anyone to build and staff such a center. She had no longstanding connection with our operations, no real firsthand experience with our programs. Why did she pick The Salvation Army?

Because it wasn't just a construction project Joan Kroc needed building. And it wasn't just a social service facility that needed managing. She had a dream of a community reconnection on a scale no one had dared imagine, including those who operated the traditional social agencies or even those who lived in the neighborhood. It was an aggressive investment in hope. And she became convinced, entirely by our reputation, that we could bring the highest return on that investment.

To fully appreciate what such a gift implies about our organizational approach, consider the new, results-oriented business environment in which choices like Mrs. Kroc's occur. When management theorists talk about challenges facing organizations in the new millennium, the rhetoric of revolution creeps into just about every conversation. "In this new age, a company that is evolving slowly is already on its way to extinction," writes strategist Gary Hamel, who named his 2000 advice book for managers *Leading the Revolution.*

Technology has shortened response times and widened networks of information. Knowledge monopolies are broken. Because of the Internet, everyone now knows what it costs to get something done and who will compete to do it. Access to the information you need to make decisions is becoming universal, which means old-style managers who thought their jobs were all about rationing service to customers and employment terms to workers are in trouble. They are relics of inward-facing organizations in a market that demands outward attention.

The old way allowed supply and managers to rule; now it's all about demand and customer satisfaction. And, says Michael Hammer, the author and former MIT professor, "when a customer calls the tune, everyone in the company must dance."

You can forget about the old presumptions of a manager's domain, says Hammer. "When the customer comes first in the environment, something has to adjust in the company culture. Customers care nothing for our management structure, our strategic plan, or our financial structure. They are interested in only one thing: results, the value we deliver."

The pace of this new environment is reflected in the near-overnight ascendancy of computer software and Internet firms, a phenomenon that undermined confidence in what used to be conventional wisdom about markets and management. The "new economy" entrepreneurs, trumpeting new paradigms for doing business, began to displace the authority of old-style corporate leaders. And for a while, the revolution seemed to be complete, as the new guys' companies posted triple-digit revenue growths and were rewarded with skyrocketing share prices. Then, in the dramatic investor pullback of 2000, *their* assumptions began looking as shaky as the ones they overthrew. The revolution just kept right on revolting.

So is everything now up for grabs?

Well, maybe not everything. And maybe much less than we think. If there were no solid ground to stand on, it would never occur to us how fast things are moving. If there were no common values, we couldn't get two people—let alone organizations with thousands of employees and millions of customers—to come to terms on anything.

Jim Collins and Jerry Porras argue that the idea that "the only constant is change" is one of the myths undercut by their analysis of visionary companies: "A visionary company almost religiously preserves its core ideology—changing it seldom, if ever. Core values in a visionary company form a rock-solid foundation and do not drift with the trends and fashions of the day . . . the basic purpose of a visionary company—its reason for being—can serve as a guiding beacon for centuries, like an enduring star on the horizon."

It's time to talk, then, about what is and what is not changing in the current environment.

What is most certainly being altered is the luxury of complacency, especially complacency rooted in out-of-date assumptions about time and geography. Thanks for the most part to communications technology, the time it takes for customers to register satisfaction or frustration is decreasing to zero. Distance is irrelevant—which means that organizations, which heretofore suffered no penalties for being slow and unapproachable, are vulnerable, and enterprises, which are responsive and intimate, enjoy new advantages.

In this new atmosphere, organizational problems become more obvious much faster. Near-instant and continuing connectiveness between customers and company and between employees and managers makes operations more transparent. People inside and outside can see what's going right and what's going wrong pretty much as it's happening. And with processes and policies exposed as never before, there are fewer places to hide.

That brings us to one of those the-more-things-change-the-more-they-stay-the-same ironies. Here we are, in this revolutionary climate in which change seems to rule; yet the importance of at least one old way of doing business is not only undiminished, its value is escalating.

Integrity has never counted for more. With everybody watching, you'd better be on track to deliver what you promise. You'd better be who you say you are.

You don't have to be seated in a church pew to hear that sermon. We're getting it regularly from the leaders of the new economy. "In the dot-com era," says Scott McNealy, cofounder, chairman, and CEO of Sun Microsystems, "trust—the direct result of integrity and reputation—remains critical. . . . The only difference now is that reputations, which still take time to build, can be tarnished more quickly. But that makes trust a more valuable commodity in the so-called virtual world."

Integrity is one of those concepts that gets talked to death. By the time we've reached adulthood, we've heard it in so many contradictory contexts that its meaning has been diluted by the repetition. Yet we still know integrity when we see it. And we value it, especially when it's anchored in practical affairs and linked with its primary attribute: accountability. To have integrity is to be accountable.

From the beginning, because of our double mission, The Salvation Army has had to be doubly accountable. To those who may not share Salvationists' religious faith, the Army must demonstrate that, in putting its spiritual purpose at the fore-front, it actually strengthens attention to clients' total wel-fare—in body, mind, and soul. To those driven by religious faith, the Army must show that it's not distracted by social services from its evangelical purpose. The Army must always prove its promise to maintain "heart to God, hand to man."

As early as 1890, Booth knew he had to justify the invest-ments of faith and material resources for which he was plead-ing; so *In Darkest England and the Way Out* is full of statistics from early Army research, demonstrating both the need and the Army's record of service in London's East End. We do the same today. Our annual reports are full of numbers as well as anec-dotes. Where we receive government contracts and grants, we willingly submit to those programs' standards of measurement. We have to show how clients benefit from our approaches. And we tend to opt for public shows of accountability, even when it costs us money—which is saying something for an organiza-tion that prides itself on parsimony.

In the mid-1990s, the Army in the United States was faced with a big decision about bookkeeping. It would make it easier for donors to compare charities, we were told, if we adopted the same accounting practices used by others in the nonprofit sector. Within our ranks, there wasn't a lot of enthusiasm for the idea, because the status quo was working fine for us. We weren't having problems keeping track of our own business. And we didn't have any trouble convincing donors we used contributions effectively.

What's more, the changeover was going to be expensive and time-consuming, requiring hundreds of thousands of dollars and years of employee time to adapt computer systems. Then, after all the hassle of making such a change, we weren't likely to know any more about our own finances than we knew under the old method. And if it turned out that there was some small element in our approach that wasn't as efficient as some other nonprofits, we would be exposed for all to see.

We committed ourselves to the conversion because, in the long run, we believed it would enhance our brand. It would remove one more barrier to transparency. It would keep us accountable and efficient. And it would be a continuing public demonstration of our determination to be who we say we are. If it exposed some shortcoming, all the better, because it would compel us to fix the problem to keep our purpose and our practice in sync.

Think of what we put on the line when we contract with government agencies for treating addicts or for monitoring the transition of prisoners back into the community. We invite others to judge our processes by their standards. Are we doing what we said we'd do? Are we increasing the likelihood these clients will be able to make it on their own? Are we better at doing that than other organizations? In the public service arena, those are questions that require answers everyone can see.

Our integrity is in the spotlight, too, when we provide disaster relief. Often, one of the first images viewers see when they tune to TV reports of the efforts to help victims of a flood or hurricane is a Salvation Army mobile service center or canteen. Officers and employees and volunteers in Salvation Army windbreakers are among the most visible on the scene. The passion behind the question in those crises is palpable: What are you doing to make a difference? And we have to demonstrate over and over that the faith we inspire is deserved, that the expectations we invite will be fulfilled.

In our kind of work, where it's impossible to provide the extra incentive of material compensation, we count on pride and the opportunity for soul satisfaction motivating our people. The fact is, no organization, no matter how lavishly they pay their people, can operate for very long without making available those intrinsic, non-material rewards. The quality of the pride within an organization depends on the clarity of the feedback from customers. And to get clear feedback, you have to make a clear promise—clear enough, in fact, to put your reputation at risk if you don't deliver.

For the world to know when you succeed, the world has to know when you fail. You can fudge your mission statement all you want with generalities about being "market-driven" and "responsive to customers," but if it's never clear what you feel responsible for, you'll never get credit for acting responsibly.

The transparent business environment makes the risk more obvious. And that's a good thing, as far as we're concerned. It focuses an organization's efforts on what it will take to succeed. If you are honest about your ambitions and about how you intend to accomplish your goals, and everyone is watching, you can't help but be zeroed in on your mission. Your reputation rides on it.

Inspiring trust is important for any organization. But it's life-and-death for a nonprofit. People invest their time and their money in institutions they believe to be honest and effective. But few take the time to look at the fine print in annual reports or to research every program and policy. They make their decisions based almost entirely upon the organization's reputation. We've found that people feel connected to us—or are at least appreciative of what they think we do—even when they don't know much about our operations.

Here's what our research tells us: When we asked people in the spring of 2000 to rank desirable attributes of charities, they rated "uses donations effectively" as the most important consideration. And those same people graded the Army very high (8 on a 10-point scale) for making the most of its resources.

The survey suggested the Army gets a great deal of credit from Americans for working hard (8.51 on the 10-point scale), being compassionate (8.31), and being tolerant (7.25). And when asked what immediately comes to mind when they think of the Army, a third of respondents volunteer something about our helping the poor and needy.

When our marketing advisors look at surveys like that, they almost always point to an anomaly: There's all this good feeling about The Salvation Army, yet relatively few folks are able to identify specific programs. For instance, only a tenth of respondents on that 2000 survey said they associate the Army with providing food for the hungry and homeless. And even fewer people identified with thrift stores and disaster relief, two of our major continuing efforts.

It's a curious combination, isn't it, high levels of appreciation, low levels of program awareness? Other organizations, especially for-profit enterprises, might spend a fortune on marketing to realize only a fraction of the good will our name enjoys. And the research suggests people don't even know what a lot of our "products" are.

What gives? If people aren't aware of everything we do, what accounts for the intensity and the persistence of their faith in us?

Here's what we suspect: We benefit collectively—we, in fact, enjoy a nationwide multiplier effect—from the individual successes of the Army's community programs. It's an aura built by millions of impressions, some earned from direct experiences in Army programs but most gained from secondhand stories of our compassion and dependability in neighborhoods we serve.

It's that simple. We are warmly viewed and supported by so many people on a nationwide basis because of the radiating effect of our performances, community by community. This is the kind of marketing that costs the least and lasts the longest. And every organization can make use of it. All that's required is performance in accord with promises.

The amazing mileage we seem to get out of this performance-as-marketing engine is probably more puzzling in an age of advertising than it might have been much earlier. Not so long ago, just about everyone connected image with reputation and reputation with performance. But over the last half-century, many people have come to believe that image-making responsibilities lie with a part of the company that's entirely separate from the part that makes products and serves customers. In fact, brand-building campaigns are often jobbed out to outside agencies, which are specialists in creating impressions for products they may have only seen momentarily—and then only because they're paid to.

There's great risk in separating these functions, of assuming that the people and the processes responsible for building and protecting the name of an institution are different from those engaged in day-to-day efforts to serve customers. Ultimately, no matter how good a marketing campaign you run, the value of your brand depends *entirely* on how you satisfy customer expectations. A brilliant ad campaign can, in fact, create problems if it invites people to experience firsthand a gap between promise and performance.

As obvious as this may seem, its implications may have been disguised by inefficiencies in the old ways of doing business, when it took a while for feedback to penetrate boundaries within and outside of the organization. In the age of transparency, though, the shields are down. Whatever advantages accrued to managers who were insulated by message-stopping barriers are no more. For any organization nowadays, ignorance and isolation are huge handicaps. And excuses for not moving to close performance gaps are seen as what they are, failures of will and competence.

In the new era, we're back to the old basics. You build trust by doing what you say you're going to do. You keep trust by staying in touch with the needs of those you serve. You must remove every obstacle that blocks the integration of your purpose and your processes. And you must inspire in your people wholehearted belief in that integration at every level.

The inspiration must come from people in the organization who embody the brand, who model the core values. The Salvation Army's first role models were its founders, William and Catherine Booth. William Booth went at his job with such fervor that, as a famous story goes, an insurance company insisted on raising his premiums unless he slowed his pace. He, of course, opted for the higher payments. Catherine Booth, by assuming an equal role in the pulpit and in service programs, set the standard for diversified leadership in the young Army. And together, the couple inspired not only a mission that became an Army but a curious world.

When William Booth died in 1912 at the age of 83, it was as if a head of state had passed away. Some 65,000 people came to view his body in state. Monarchs sent wreaths. Behind the funeral cortege, 5,000 Salvationists marched six abreast.

The Booth charisma passed to some of his children, especially to daughter Evangeline, who was born the year her father founded the movement in 1865. She clearly had her parents' gifts for inspiring crowds and building unlikely coalitions. And she used those powers to the fullest when she took over the Army in America in 1904.

Like her father, Evangeline Booth put a face on the Army for the public at large. In widely attended public presentations in which she made full use of all sorts of theatrical costuming and staging techniques, she dramatized the plight of the poor and hungry for audiences that might never have sat still for a sermon. By sheer force of personality and attention-grabbing events, she raised levels of identification with the Army in the United States. And she built coalitions of support among the wealthy and the well-connected, who helped fund programs and broadened the Army's reach. "From 1905 to 1934," writes Diane Winston, "Evangeline Booth was the single most important weapon in the Army's struggle to define itself."

Of course, it wasn't just The Salvation Army struggling to define its organizational approaches during that period. America itself was undergoing a radical transition to prominence. World War I and the Great Depression occurred on Evangeline Booth's watch as national commander. And like The Salvation Army, drawn by its mission into the heart of the traumas, the America that was forced to cope with those trials was reshaped by the experience.

While it might never have occurred to those who were caught up in those times and who relied on a larger-than-life leader like Evangeline Booth to inspire the troops within and rally financial support from without, the era of war and Depression was beginning to impose a new sense of reality on decision-makers. It, too, was a time of revolution.

The world in the opening decades of the twentieth century was larger and more complicated than the one leaders of the Victorian era had been born into. It would require new levels of expertise and broader approaches to problem solving. And organizations intending to grow in that complex swirl were going to have to evolve styles of leadership and methods of operation that moved away from the charismatic and autocratic, and toward the systematic and democratic—which is one of the reasons Winston is right when she says Evangeline Booth was "a public figure and newsmaker as no other American Salvationist before or since."

We're going to talk in detail in the next section about this transition in leadership style. For our purpose here, though, we should note this irony: The founding general's most famous daughter, who became the international general herself in 1934, represented the high-water mark of charismatic leadership in The Salvation Army. Yet, even though she might not have been aware of it at the time, she did much to speed the Army's transition to an era in which it would grow even larger, even more effective, and even more influential without relying on the personal appeal of its commander.

Evangeline Booth successfully resisted efforts at headquarters in England—including efforts of her brother, Bramwell, when he was general—to tighten controls on American Salvationists, thus allowing them to make adaptations to American culture that made them seem more like homegrown social evangelists than an invading force. Her connections among the rich and influential, from pioneer retailer John Wanamaker to banker E.F. Hutton, helped her establish a tradition of high-profile fund-raisers and build a firm foundation beneath Army finances in America. But most important of all from a brand-building point of view was her idea to send women Salvationists close to the European front lines during World War I to serve food and to provide a sense of family support for American soldiers.

Those female Salvationists became known as "Sallies." In tents and huts erected as close to the front lines as they were allowed, the women baked donuts, served coffee, darned socks, and listened to lonely soldiers as substitute sisters and mothers. They also led devotional services and prayers and sang familiar hymns with the men. They were, in short, links with family and faith in times that threatened to separate the soldiers from both.

Like the Army's services everywhere, the Sallies' helping hands were extended without discrimination. "Even atheists and members of other religious traditions appreciated the

Salvationists' hospitality," writes Winston, "which included allowing members of other groups to use the huts. Fraternal orders held meetings there, Jews and Catholics conducted services, and divisional bands gathered for practice."

And the Sallies, like their sister and brother soldiers in cities back home, went out of their way to connect themselves to those, quite literally, on the front lines. "The Army's popularity sprang not only from what it did but from what it was," Winston continues. "Salvationists made it clear that they served the enlisted men, not the officers. Accepting no favors from the brass, Salvationists slept, ate, and worked under the same conditions as the doughboys. Not surprisingly, infantrymen considered the Salvationists their own."

Returning soldiers couldn't say enough about the contributions of the Sallies. Poems and songs about them found their way into the popular culture. Posters and magazine covers elevated them to near-sainthood. And not even Evangeline Booth, with all her gifts for marketing, could have imagined when she initiated the program the bonus the Army would get from it.

The Sallies were real people, not the creations of a public-relations campaign. Yet their personal—and relatively anonymous—exemplification of Army purposes and methods connected The Salvation Army with the public as no charismatic leader could. The Sallies projected an image of selfless service, even in the face of extreme danger, and inspired almost universal appreciation. And best of all, it was an accurate interpretation of what they really did. The Army got one of the world's great image-making opportunities merely by attending to business, by delivering what we promise.

As The Salvation Army expanded in the days after the World Wars, its image has become even less dependent on charismatic leadership. The most recognizable symbols of our work are the Army shield, the Christmas kettles, and our officers' and soldiers' uniforms.

In an age of individuality, of celebrating diversity and entrepreneurial vigor, uniforms, to some people, suggest conformity, a certain rigidity of mind. Many people say they'd feel restricted, even oppressed, if they had to wear a uniform every day. For Army officers, however, the opposite is true. We are what we are most proud of when we wear the Army uniform. It's a real timesaver, too. It says: "This is who we are." No introduction necessary.

When William Booth began the Army in nineteenth-century England, the advantages of uniforms were obvious. Wearing distinctive dress immediately established an identity for a group that depended upon public recognition. Uniforms also tapped into Victorian pride for the Army of the Empire. They implied courage, discipline, and professionalism. So, Booth reasoned, if The Salvation Army was to be taken seriously, it should be a uniformed Army.

There were also practical considerations. For the poor recruited to service, uniforms removed the stigma of ragged dress. For the well to do, they symbolized a willingness to do away with worldly concerns about fashion finery. Uniforms helped democratize the movement.

Those practical considerations still exist. When we wear the Army uniform, we are demonstrating in appearance as well as philosophy that we are all cut from the same cloth. But what's even more important, after more than 135 years of Army influence around the world, is the symbolic continuity of the uniform, its ability to inspire in us and in others recognition of our purpose.

When Army officers travel, they are invariably stopped in airports and in train stations, in public places of all kinds, by people with stories to tell or prayers to request. These people have specific memories of the Salvation Army uniform entering their lives at crucial moments. It could have been a youth coach or a bandleader or a League of Mercy visitor in the hospital. It could have been the officer who offered hot coffee and warm blankets in the aftermath of a flood or a hurricane. It may have been a counselor in a rehab center or an officer who reunited missing family members. So many people have had life-altering experiences with someone in our uniform that wearing it links us to our past and to the people we serve now. It's terrific, cost-effective advertising.

There's no reason other organizations can't get a similar advantage from a public declaration of who they are. It's not a matter of putting on a particular set of clothes. It's about manifesting the principles of the organization for all to see. You wear your values. You model the mission. You declare your accountability.

We can't tell you how many beneficiaries have entered our programs, how many life-long volunteers were initially attracted, how many employees and officers were recruited by the examples Salvation Army officers set. But that's the outward-facing, public-relations value of "wearing the uniform." Think how important that image is inside of our organization. Seeing the way others react to our brand puts responsibility on all of us to continue measuring up. We have to keep doing business with the integrity, with the commitment to mission, that the tradition symbolizes.

Employees in businesses feel the same surges of pride and obligation when customers respond to company products or when media coverage lauds a company's approach. The stories that are most attractive to news organizations and have the most impact inside a company are not about money. They're about how a company faced and overcame a particularly daunting challenge or chose a responsible path when it may have been more profitable in the short run to do otherwise.

Corporate team members who see their project from research and development to production to marketing and, finally, to sales, often talk about how excited they get when they see the first ad in a magazine or on television: "That's what we've been working on all this time," they say.

You have to make the most of the link between pride and performance by continually clearing away the stuff that interferes with people connecting what they do in the organization with how it's received on the outside. That's why we keep sending out desk-bound officers and employees to experience programs and to talk to beneficiaries firsthand.

You'll see staff people handing out cups of coffee in disaster relief efforts. And you'll no doubt spot some of our computer programmers and office managers on volunteer duty with Army programs in their communities. Everybody has to sense the effect of their labors on end users. They have to hear the cheers and jeers themselves. When they do, it makes it easier for them to commit to behaving in ways that continue to earn the respect of others and continue to inspire the pride they feel in themselves.

Here's an important thing about that kind of pride. You can't "instill" it in an organization, as we so often hear. Pride is earned. It grows from performance in line with expectations everybody agrees on. And you risk losing the bonus pride affords an organization when you let your practices slip out of alignment with your purpose, no matter how compellingly you advertise your intentions. The first to notice the misalignment, even before customers, will be employees.

We've already talked about the need all of us have to feel connected to some meaningful purpose in our lives. When we join organizations, we bring that need with us. And it's such a powerful need that most people will look to salvage some pleasure in performance regardless of whether or not an organization is diligent about keeping promises and whether or not managers support employee efforts.

Too often in too many companies, the best people feel as if they have to overcome company-induced or company-tolerated barriers—rigid policies, out-of-date procedures, and stifling layers of decision-making—in order to accomplish worthy goals. Some develop tricks for evading managers who stifle them. Some conspire with others to do work they can be proud of in spite of what *they*—the suits and the numbers-crunchers—put in their way. That turns high performance into a subversive act and drives a wedge of cynicism between managers and workers. And that's very dangerous business.

Managers, even in good companies, who can't or won't model the best values of the organization in their relationships with employees, threaten its most important resource—access to talent. Good people avoid bad managers. They'll leave an organization they like, even one they're proud of, if they don't respect their bosses or feel respected by them. And the ones who stick around are less productive than they would be if they were inspired and committed.

"It's really pretty basic," said one executive quoted in an *American Demographics* study of the effect of employee-management relations on productivity and profits. "Even if you work for a good company, if you have a lousy boss, you have a lousy job."

If employees believe they have lousy jobs, they're less committed to the work. And to no one's surprise, organizations with less committed people perform at lower levels than those with folks who buy into the organization's core principles and connect with those principles through the organization's leaders. And it's not just the guys in the top of the organizational chart who have to be good managers. The evidence suggests that immediate supervisors are often the most influential factors of all.

For 25 years, the Gallup Organization gathered data on the priorities of the most productive workers in a wide range of organizations. The conclusions were the basis of a 1999 book by Marcus Buckingham and Curt Coffman, *First, Break All the*

Rules: What the World's Greatest Managers Do Differently. "Our research yielded many discoveries," say the authors in their introduction, "but the most powerful was this: Talented employees need great managers. The talented employee may join a company because of its charismatic leaders, its generous benefits, and its world-class training programs, but how long that employee stays and how productive he is while he is there is determined by his relationship with his immediate supervisor."

Ultimately, then, even if your organization has a worthy vision and a product the market is likely to embrace, you can put everything at risk by not modeling your values consistently— not only for your customers *out there* but also for your people inside. "Think of it as kneading bread," say James C. Collins and William C. Lazier, "constantly massaging the values into the essence of the organization."

So the answer to the question about what put us in the position to be considered for Joan Kroc's generosity in San Diego has multiple levels: We earned the opportunity because of our reputation. Our reputation is built on our determination to achieve the highest possible levels of effectiveness. That effectiveness depends on our ability to align our purpose continually with our processes throughout the organization, which requires acting consistently with integrity in all our relationships.

If we can do that, we gain spectacular practical advantages, not only in representing ourselves to the public but in managing the nuts and bolts of our daily operations. It's a management aid, focusing us on the promises we make to all our partners outside and inside of the organization. It has everything to do with the bottom line in our business. In plenty of others, too.

If you were looking for a demonstration of the need for integrity in the for-profit sector, look to one of the most frenzied marketplaces you can imagine: the stock market, specifically Nasdaq, which has become the United States' largest stock market in dollar volume.

In 1994, after allegations of sloppy practices and questionable behavior on the part of Nasdaq dealers, the U.S. Justice Department and the Securities and Exchange Commission launched investigations of the high-tech market. Over the next two years, in response to the government inquiries, Nasdaq undertook a major housecleaning. It upgraded its system for handling trades, insuring security, and enforcing rules. And it revamped its management structure.

Among the new people brought in to oversee the changes and inspire new levels of trust in the public was Alfred R. Berkeley III, who had been instrumental, as a securities analyst specializing in technology, in helping to put together the initial public offerings of companies such as the Microsoft Corp. and Oracle Systems Corp. Berkeley became Nasdaq president in mid-1996 and immediately began talking tough about building trust.

Nasdaq systems had to be fast and dependable, said Berkeley. Its rules had to be clear and rigidly enforced. Traders who tried to manipulate those rules, he said, should "be thrown out of the business."

Berkeley, who has since become vice-chairman of Nasdaq, thinks integrity is what holds the whole thing together: "Nasdaq is all about mutually advantageous transactions among strangers. We move billions of dollars daily in electronic markets because we can, by and large, trust the companies to be what they say they are; we can trust the markets to deal with our orders in a fair and predictable way; and we can trust the intermediaries to whom we send cash and negotiable securities to deliver as promised and to be solvent."

Expressed that way, it's hard to argue against the idea of trust as a precursor to any successful business relationship, whether the business takes place via an electronic stock exchange or at the greengrocer's. In fact, it's essential to any human relationship. Having integrity, being consistently trustworthy, turns out to be one of the most practical habits we can acquire.

"It just makes good sense," says Berkeley. "It's a good way to live your life. And it's pragmatic. You get better results."

And it may turn out to be the best thing to hold onto when the next revolution comes. Iain Somerville, founder and managing partner of the Andersen Consulting Center for Thought Leadership, and John Edwin Mroz, founder and president of the Institute for EastWest Studies, have been advisors to leaders of global for-profit enterprises and heads of state. To connect successfully with the next generation of citizens, customers, and workers, say Somerville and Mroz, you must demonstrate the alignment of personal and organizational integrity. You have to embody the principles you say you stand for: "Capturing the hearts and minds of Generation X'ers and Z'ers will require an even greater commitment to worthwhile purposes. Organizations must forge a new relationship with their world that goes beyond mere competitiveness. They need to be purposeful in ways that resonate with the people they touch and to access levels of performance that go beyond the ordinary. This purpose is not so much a mission or goal as a commitment made visible in the day-to-day behavior of people throughout the organization."

5

LEAD BY LISTENING

To grow from a start-up to a much larger enterprise, to thrive over the long term without losing either mission focus or creative energy, requires skills that aren't nearly so apparent or crucial when an organization launches. In fact, they may be skills that are quite the opposite of those required to get off the ground.

These new skills must be mastered and institutionalized, built into the structure of the organization so they can be perpetuated. In the next chapter, we'll talk about what the Army has learned about building and maintaining such structures. Here, however, we want to concentrate on the core competency that precedes and envelops the others: Listening with the intent to learn and with the commitment to act.

The promise to listen is like the pledge to act with integrity. It's recited so often, even in situations that contradict the words as they come out of the speaker's mouth, that it's often ignored. What manager doesn't swear that "the door is always open"?

Ultimately, the test for listening is response. You must prove you're paying attention by how you act on the information you get. But before you reach that moment, to get the most out of listening opportunities, you must accept the egalitarian premise that underlies the process.

The deepest, most rewarding kind of listening implies a relationship. It is not merely a tool or a strategy. It's a way of looking at the world. In The Salvation Army, in fact, we believe there's a theological dimension to listening. It goes to the heart of our "theology of service."

We believe God created all of us with a need to reach out to others by Jesus' example. All human lives are connected and approach the wholeness they aspire to only when they are aligned with God's purpose—which means all humans are potential partners in the effort toward reconciliation with divine purpose. We're all part of the same family, equals in God's eyes, regardless of our temporary stations as service providers or service recipients, as managers or as employees. And it goes against that conviction to listen to others with condescending or manipulative motives.

Since we're all in this together, we need to hear and understand one another continually. Blocking the flow of information is like blocking the flow of blood. It threatens the very life of our relationships and our organizations, which is why we consider listening, both in the personal and in the organizational sense, a fundamental survival skill.

This idea that an organization is like a living organism "isn't just a semantic or academic issue," argues Arie de Geus, the former Royal Dutch/Shell executive and management theorist. "It has enormous practical, day-to-day implications for managers. It means that, in a world that changes massively, many times, during the course of your career, you need to involve people in the continued development of the company. The amount that people care, trust, and engage themselves at work has not only a direct effect on your bottom line, but the most direct effect, of any factor, on your company's expected lifespan. The fact that many companies ignore this imperative is one of the great tragedies of our times."

All organizations struggle at one time or another with ways to get fresh perspectives, to engage new people, in decision-making. The Salvation Army was barely a quarter-century old when it experienced its first leadership crisis.

Our founder, William Booth, was unusual for church leaders of his era in that he saw great potential in people who were hurting. He listened intently, heard their needs, and responded with a passion that helped define our movement. In other ways, however, Booth was a product of his times, times in which the monarchy and the military provided the dominant models for managing organizations. As far as many of his contemporaries were concerned, The Salvation Army was William Booth's Army. And as everyone knew, especially during the heady days of Britain's world empire, an army was nothing if not disciplined by unquestioning obedience through a chain of command, with a supreme commander at the top.

That autocratic style suited Booth. But as the Army expanded from its base in England, the disadvantages of a military-style organization commanded entirely from a London headquarters became more and more obvious. Officers on the front lines in distant lands were no less inspired by mission than were leaders back home in England. New "customers" were no less responsive to the message. But it was getting harder to operate strictly by the Founder's script in new territories and even tougher to negotiate thorny issues with a supreme command across the ocean. Not surprisingly, matters came to a head in America, where the English-born commander, Major Thomas E. Moore, found himself torn between the demands of a new foreign command and obedience to the founding general.

The cultural rift turned into a legal divide over the purely technical issue of incorporation. The Army in America was beginning to build an enterprise that consisted of real estate, bank accounts, and other assets and liabilities. And unless it was incorporated as an American company, the law made the Army's top ranking officer in this country—Major Moore—responsible for it all. Booth, however, refused to authorize a move that, as far as he was concerned, diminished his mandate to do God's work.

Major Moore, not known for either administrative acumen or diplomatic skills, didn't help matters. He had difficulty explaining his position to London and fell increasingly out of favor. Booth ordered Moore to South Africa and appointed a new commander in his place in 1884. But Moore refused to go and rallied troops loyal to him, incorporated a rival Salvation Army of America, and tried to run it as an organization ideologically identical to, but operationally independent from, the one that arrived in Battery Park under The Salvation Army flag four years before.

The problem was a classic one in organizational development. It revealed an attention deficit at the top. William Booth was paying rapt attention to the voice inside him that argued for focus and control—a voice, by the way, that had guided him and the Army through desperate times. But he was so tuned to that inner voice he couldn't hear compelling evidence from the outside that changes were necessary in some of the organization's *means* if it were to continue to serve its *ends*.

In Booth's mind, the Army's mission and his means were inseparable. Both were products of a vision he saw as divinely inspired and dependent upon his authority. And by his way of thinking, a challenge to his way of doing business was an assault on the business itself, on the Army's sacred purpose.

The Moore split could have meant disaster. As it was, it took five years to fix. It might have taken longer if Moore had been a better manager. But from the beginning, his shortcomings threatened his operation's solvency and frustrated junior officers' efforts to make a go of secession. In 1889, his own board of trustees deposed and replaced him.

But there were two other factors that had even more to do with putting things back together again. One was Booth's decision to finally signal that he was paying attention to America. He made his first trip to this country in the fall and winter of 1886–87. And the power of the veteran evangelist to attract media attention and to inspire loyalists worked its wonders. Booth, says Army historian Edward H. McKinley, "was cheered, adored, quoted—and believed. The decline of Moore's troops became precipitate."

The other factor was the determination of key officers on both sides of the split to work things out. Most believed that despite disagreements on how to manage the movement, its mission still united them. Moore's successor among the secessionists almost immediately began talking informally with Booth loyalists. Ballington Booth, the general's son and national commander in the United States beginning in 1887, welcomed the idea of reunification. And the two sides moved closer together until there was a formal reconciliation in 1889.

How different was William Booth's listening problem from that of many managers today? Not very. In theory, we all believe leaders should have their ears to the ground for approaching change, for seismic shifts in the marketplace. But if you look closely at how information actually finds its way to decision-makers in real-life organizations, you'd see something else entirely.

Many operations allow systems to develop that severely attenuate influences from the outside, "purifying" incoming information until it's irrelevant. People in the field suspect they'll be blamed if feedback contradicts managers' assumptions, so they avoid hearing customers' complaints. Or even worse, they withhold information from headquarters for fear of frustrating expectations.

Junior managers engrained in the corporate culture learn to stifle their dissent. Everybody gets in the habit of saying what they think *they*—the people in the executive suites—want to hear. And the whole operation becomes increasingly cut off from the environment in which it's doing business.

General Booth sent emissaries to the United States to investigate Major Moore's concerns, but they knew the Founder's disposition well enough to know what he wanted to hear. And that's what they were predisposed to see in America. The general's representatives found it far easier to blame the U.S. commander's lack of organizational skills for the dilemma than to grasp the true legal issue or to understand resistance to another form of "taxation without representation"—requiring blind obedience to rules front-line troops had no hope of influencing. The emissaries certainly weren't going to go back to the general and report anything from which he could infer criticism. So the future of the whole enterprise was put at risk.

When authentic feedback is prevented from influencing an organization's direction, it can't adapt or grow. It is literally without its senses. In giant organizations, the sensory deprivation is subtle and complex. There are more layers of information management, of spin and counter-spin. Elaborate rituals of avoidance and forgetting evolve. It takes longer for the inevitable to become apparent, but the death spiral is the same. The life span of most organizations—especially organizations in highly competitive environments—is relatively short. All are born with a certain invigorating awareness. They stop paying attention, stop reacting to their environment. And they begin to die.

To avoid that cycle, an organization must listen, learn, and adapt like the living organism de Geus describes. That "living organization" theory is connected to a larger one, the "learning organization" movement that has caught on with many business thinkers over the last 30 years or so. "At the heart of the learning organization," says Peter Senge, one of the movement's leading theorists, "is a shift of mind—from seeing ourselves as separate from the world to connected to the world, from seeing problems as caused by someone or something 'out there' to seeing how our own actions create the problems we experience. A learning organization is a place where people are continually discovering how they create their reality. And how they can change it."

In the Army, our mission to spread God's message and to serve without discrimination is inviolate. But we are free to reinvent—we may, in fact, be required to reinvent—just about everything else. The enthusiasm for reinvention has to come from the people we serve and work with. And the only way to nurture that creativity, to maintain a living, learning organization, is to take great pains to cultivate an environment in which they can speak honestly and we can listen non-critically.

In the years since William Booth, The Salvation Army has evolved a structure—a system of power sharing among voting commissioners and prominent advisory boards—that dilutes the pure autocratic power of one individual, even if he or she is the international general. But that doesn't mean we can afford to stop amending and adapting our processes to ensure that the life blood of information keeps reaching decision-makers—and that decision-makers keep validating those processes by acting on what they hear.

Here's an adaptation we made in the 1990s when we sensed we were allowing a communications gap to grow between our National Advisory Board and senior officers at the territorial level. These two groups represent powerful influences on the national policies of The Salvation Army. The officers who command the four territories, together with the national commander, comprise the Commissioners Conference, the ruling body of uniformed officers in America. The National Advisory

Board is composed of prominent "movers and shakers," many of them longtime Army volunteers and donors who help us broaden our perspectives and expand our networks of support.

NAB members come aboard knowing they can only advise us, not set policy, because that role is left primarily to The Salvation Army's Board of Trustees and to the Commissioners Conference. But if we can't demonstrate we are not only listening to what our advisors suggest, but are willing to change what we do in response to their best ideas, then we'll lose them to some other organization that can better appreciate and reward their commitment.

For some time, territorial commanders and key members of their staffs had been invited to attend NAB meetings, but they didn't actively participate in board members' discussions out of respect for the independent function of this distinguished panel. The panel is so distinguished, in fact, full of CEOs and former CEOs of powerful companies, that some of our officers probably felt more comfortable in the background.

Our NAB members, however, didn't value their independence nearly so much as their ability to have an impact. And they wanted to know why it was taking so long for their recommendations to work their way into Army operations. The answer was that some of the suggestions had problems that only officers with certain kinds of field experience could have foreseen. Some ideas had to be modified. Some were entirely unworkable.

Here's what sent up alarms: Veterans among the staff people observing those NAB meetings may have spotted some of the hitches in proposals while the advisors were preparing to recommend them. But out of deference to the NAB, they didn't speak up, even though they knew that they or others would have to alter or kill off the ideas down the line.

Unconsciously, we had created a system that inhibited learning by blocking constructive discussion. So we fixed it. We made it clear that senior officers attending the NAB sessions were expected to engage the members in the discussions. And we assigned territorial staffers to NAB committees so there was an experienced voice in the room at the earliest stages of idea discussions.

What happened almost immediately is that the time it took for an NAB recommendation to have an impact diminished. Officers could comfortably take ownership of proposals because they were parties to them. They became advocates rather than road blocks. Frustration levels declined for both NAB members and senior officers. And whatever cynicism we had allowed to creep into the system dissipated as well. That's what purposeful listening will do for an organization.

If we needed models for listening, we'd do well to stick to those we've created over time at the program level. People come to us hungry or homeless or trapped in addiction. They can't pay the electric bill or daycare fees for their children. They don't know how to get medical help for their families. And they feel desperate, depressed, often paralyzed by the obstacles.

Many of them have already experienced the humiliation of asking for aid from people in authority who view them with contempt. They don't have to hear the words. They hear it in the impatient tones of voice or in the body language of people who just want them to disappear, to stop draining the resources of the productive sector of society. They are reminded constantly of how they have fallen short, how they lack the will— or even the capability—to change, which means, for many of them, the kind of listening they've experienced so far has only aggravated their paralysis and hardened their cynicism.

When we listen, however, it's from a perspective informed by our faith. Since we believe we are all made of the same stuff, that no one is inherently deficient in what it takes to change, we're looking for opportunities to assist the transformation. The hurting people before us are temporarily blocked from making the connections—especially, we believe, the spiritual connection—that will allow them to operate in full partnership with God's purpose. They just need help unblocking themselves.

We're listening for possibilities, not limitations. We're looking for traits that may be undeveloped or misdirected but that hold the secret for future fulfillment—and for contributions they can make to others' lives. It's not their need that defines our customers; rather, it's their untapped capacity for performance in accord with the larger purpose we all share. We can't know their potential contribution without paying attention to each of them individually. And we can't activate that potential unless we demonstrate we're willing to use our organization to help them recognize opportunities to become their best selves. When we can, we create those opportunities.

The classic Salvation Army example of that process is that of Michael Roland, who by the time he was 36 years old, had been struggling with drug and alcohol addictions for 20 years. He'd done time in jail for drug-related offenses and committed other crimes to support his habit. That's a record bad enough to be considered a lost cause in the minds of many people. Maybe in Roland's mind, too, because he was living on the Detroit streets in the winter of 1989, at risk of freezing in the 25-degree-below-zero nights, when Meals on Wheels volunteers discovered him.

They immediately stopped their route in order to take him to the Harbor Light Center—the same center in Detroit that so inspired Alice and me at that Easter service some eight years later. "I really surrendered," remembers Roland. "They let me know I was loved. But for the first time in my life I was held accountable."

His new mentors saw beyond Roland's problems to the potential within him. Here was a man who had lived by his wits but had misdirected his talents for so many years. "I didn't believe in myself," Roland says. "I wasn't comfortable with success. If I ever made any money, it created a problem for me. So I became good at being broke. My addictions kept me that way."

As he got help to control his appetites for drugs, Roland also learned through Army programs how to make healthier decisions about other aspects of his life, including building supportive relationships and managing his resources. "For the first time, I began to feel responsible for my own life," he says. "I started taking care of myself. I got an apartment. I paid my bills. I learned how to live below my means and to budget my money."

Army leaders who watched Roland come alive in rehabilitation got him a job working in an Army corrections program and inspired him to think about ways he could hone his natural leadership skills. He became director of transitional housing. Eventually, with advice and encouragement of divisional officers, Roland applied to officer training school and was accepted.

From the time he was commissioned in 1994, Roland has used the qualities Army staffers in Michigan spotted in him years before to build and expand Army programs. "I went to major corporations on my own," he says. "I shared my story. I found I have a great skill in raising money."

Now, Roland's a captain and the administrator of the Army's Adult Rehabilitation Center in Carpenteria, California, and chaplain of the Santa Barbara County Sheriff's Department. These days, he's in the position to be the talent spotter, the mentor of others. "I have learned," he says, "how important it is to get quality people. I want to empower the next stage of leadership."

Even for managers of organizations with different products and services than The Salvation Army's, there's an important lesson here. What manager is not interested in ways "to empower the next stage of leadership"? Where so many enterprises go wrong is in concentrating their attentiveness on the wrong set of qualities in their people. Too often, in annual reviews and in other personnel evaluations, they put the energy into identifying shortcomings instead of nurturing strengths. Managers think they're being constructive in an evaluation when they say, "Here are the three things you need to improve to be more effective." But what employees often hear is, "These are the three things I think are most wrong with you." How is that conversation going to be productive?

One of the central responsibilities of leaders is picking the right people for the job. They must listen closely for evidence that a person, first of all, has the ability to achieve results in the role the leader has in mind; and, secondly, that the candidate will bring enthusiasm to the job. Under-performance by a worker means a manager guessed wrong on one or both counts.

If performance lags and the only response of the boss is to shift the entire blame to the worker, it's a partial abdication of leadership. What the manager is really saying is this: "It looks like I made a mistake in picking you to do this. But can you make it better by changing yourself to accommodate my bad judgment?"

There's a far more efficient way to go about assigning people to jobs and inspiring them to work at their highest capacity. But it requires rapt attention to candidates' strengths before and during the job assignment rather than to their deficits after they've fallen short.

You listen for evidence of what people are good at and what they enjoy (which is often the same thing), even when they don't appreciate their own talents. And you put them in roles that will reward those talents and inspire them to perform at ever higher levels. As we in the Army see over and over again with people like Michael Roland, when you listen for strengths, help develop those strengths, then back them with your organization's resources and continuing encouragement, your faith can be rewarded many times over.

Let's say you've done that and you're still not getting the results you want. What does the evidence tell you? Were you wrong about the match between the job's requirements and the individual's capabilities? Maybe the job's too easy and unchallenging. Maybe it's too hard. Either way, it doesn't match their strengths. So you give them a new assignment that does.

The Salvation Army is like most other large organizations. We have all sorts of jobs. Some require highly developed pastoral skills, where our people meet one-on-one as counselors with victims of heart-breaking tragedy. Some jobs demand back-of-the-house expertise in planning or logistics and less direct contact with the front lines. Some are for people who are especially good at finance or fund-raising or coaching or playing in a band. All have overlapping responsibilities of being a Christian leader and a compassionate service provider. But what a waste of time it would be to insist that everyone develop each of the specialties we draw upon to an equal level. We'd get bogged down in remedial training programs, trying to get the cornet players up to speed with the computer programmers, sacrificing the chance to be exceptional in so many individual situations in order to be average in all of them.

Yet some companies spend too much of their energy doing exactly that, obsessing over under-performance by people who don't have the aptitude or the interest in the jobs they're assigned. Companies have to provide training and coaching, surely, but always with the idea of opening opportunities and accelerating success rather than fixing bad choices made by inattentive managers.

When I was a leader at the divisional, territorial, and national levels of the Army, there were inevitably officers in my commands who were especially good at their primary roles but not nearly so good at other parts of their responsibilities. There were wonderful numbers specialists who had trouble communicating with other people, and there were compassionate counselors who had trouble keeping up with the paper work. I tried to coach them on little improvements in areas where they struggled that could make their lives easier. I helped them find employees or volunteers who could fill in the gaps. Or I assigned officers with complementary abilities to help them. Often, there were husband-and-wife officer teams whose specialties and dispositions meshed perfectly.

Now, what if your problem doesn't seem to be an issue of talent? The evidence tells you the job matches the person's strengths. The worker insists he or she likes the job. Yet results are sub-par. In many companies, this is the point at which a manager forces an employee into a defensive posture with a list of "areas in which you can improve." The only party expected to do any listening in that case is the employee branded as an underachiever.

But if you really do see an organization as a collaboration of people committed to a common purpose, then the leader's invitation to talk about improving performance has to go something like this: "When you took this assignment, we all agreed on goals, strategies, and time lines. At the moment, we're not getting the results we expected. What do we need to do to get on track?"

This cannot be a trick question or a disguised indictment. It must be a sincere attempt to learn something by listening. Leave open all the possibilities: Together, you might have misconceived the task; maybe you, as the manager, haven't supplied enough support; perhaps the employee has a personal problem that has to be solved before he or she can give the job full attention. You listen for opportunities to clear the path to high performance. And you listen with the mutual understanding that, together, you'll act on those opportunities.

Clearly, parties to such a conversation have to trust one another. And the only way you can get that kind of trust is to nurture it consistently in all the conversations between junior and senior members of an organization. In The Salvation Army, we try to build it into our structure.

When cadets complete their two years of training, they're commissioned as captains and assigned to jobs, often in smaller corps where they can get an immediate taste for the diversity of their responsibilities. For the next five years, these new officers—many of them husband-and-wife teams—participate in specially designed seminars, retreats, and training programs to increase their skill levels and to help them cope with the stress of their evolving duties.

Continuing education and regular personal and professional check-ins are planned throughout an officer's career. But the programs are more frequent and intense during those first five years, a period we know to be critical. It's a time when they'll establish habits that will last their whole careers. And we want the mix of challenge and support, of variety and continuity, to be right, because it will be the base they'll build on. It is very likely that most officers who make it past those five years will serve for life in The Salvation Army.

Besides the formal training, there are also continuing conversations going on at the corps and divisional levels between junior and senior people. Because most of the staff the junior officers report to have been in appointments similar to those the new folks hold, very likely in the same region, a certain amount of two-way communication is assured. Our senior people have to stay in touch with those they supervise, and the junior ones, who want to avoid wasting energy and resources, are anxious to tap into the experience of those who came before.

Two things increase the likelihood of close collaboration between junior and senior people in The Salvation Army. First of all, we've organized ourselves so that almost all of the people, money, and capital assets of the Army are invested in programs initiated and run with enormous latitude by officers and employees in communities closest to those we serve. Our focus is on the front lines. Senior staff officers spend very little time "commanding" those in the field. Instead, they support them with administrative and technical expertise and with access to regional and national resources. So the success of community programs depends on the clarity of communication between local leaders and those at headquarters. There's a built-in incentive to talk honestly and to listen intently.

The other advantage we have is our constant awareness of the gap between what we're committed to accomplish and what we have to work with. Need always exceeds resources. So we can't afford not to make the most of supportive relationships between our people. We need every bit of the wisdom of our veterans and all the energy of our young people.

I remember when I was an impulsive young captain in New York City. For some reason, I let myself get dragged into a trivial territorial dispute over the sales of the Army's *War Cry* magazines. A fellow from another corps would walk right by our office every day to sell the magazine in our area, competing with our own sales people. I tried reasoning with him, and I tried ordering him. But he ignored me. And I suppose he got under my skin.

In desperation, I dashed off a letter to our divisional commander, Lt. Col. Ken Howarth, saying I was ready to call the police on this man if he persisted on trespassing into our territory. I'll never forget the letter he sent back: "My dear captain," he wrote. "We'll resolve our family differences without the assistance of judicial authorities."

Lt. Col. Howarth had a close, fatherly relationship with all of us young officers. He probably had 75 to 100 officers under him, yet he made us feel as if we each had a personal relationship with him. He visited in our homes. He counseled us professionally and personally. He listened.

His letter back to me could have been a reprimand for getting my priorities out of whack. But the atmosphere he'd established as a leader was one in which I felt free to vent and one in which he could apply subtle influence with the tone of his voice. As soon as I read the words, I knew I'd let this small matter consume far too much of my concern. I got my perspective back. But while I may have felt a little embarrassed at raising the issue with him, Lt. Col. Howarth was so gentle in his response that I felt none of the humiliation I might have felt by a dressing-down I probably deserved.

When I became a leader of younger officers, I remembered experiences from mentors such as Lt. Col. Howarth, and I tried to perpetuate that culture of trust and caring. One of the ways I worked at that was in the tone of communications from headquarters to the field. For instance, as a divisional commander, I got copies of letters from my staff to corps officers responding to the junior officers' requests for help or for the go-ahead on pet programs. Even when we had to turn down projects, I wanted my people to make sure they explained in detail why requests were denied. And I wanted to make sure the language implied an attitude of collaboration and concern, and not a presumption of aloof authority.

For our systems to work, we need everyone working with enthusiasm toward our common purpose. We can't afford the energy drain of doubt or suspicion. So we can't be insensitive to our people's ambitions. Those officers on the front lines shouldn't read anything into the responses of their commanders that makes them think twice about proposing another idea. If we want them to keep talking, we have to prove we're always listening.

This sharing between senior and junior people, like the covenant we sign as officers, is in place for a lifetime. I stayed in touch with my mentors throughout my career. Now, in retirement, I still talk regularly with friends who once served on staffs I commanded. We're always counseling one another. In some regions, retiree mentoring is institutionalized, with retired officers "adopting" a younger one to pray for and to advise.

All this talking back and forth in the Army is not strictly about how to balance a budget or acquire a new van for the community center. Like all members of all organizations, our people bring to work with them concerns about their families. They worry about daycare issues, medical problems, education expenses, care for aging parents, and the effects the pressures of their jobs have on the people they love. In the course of career evaluation processes at most companies, these kinds of subjects bubble to the surface in honest discussions between employees and supervisors, but there's pressure not to consider them as relevant to work issues unless they reach a crisis stage. There's family life and work life. Two separate worlds.

But, as we've already stressed, we're not big believers in compartmentalizing human lives. We believe it's a waste of time to try to separate who we are at home from who we are at the office. And given The Salvation Army's preoccupation with strengthening families and communities, how true could we be to our core principles if we weren't listening and responding to our own people's concerns about their marriages and their families?

So we make those issues part of every decision about where an officer will be assigned and what job he or she will do. We talk with them about their relationships with their spouses. Are both husband and wife finding fulfillment in their assignments? Is one or the other so overloaded with work that they're too exhausted to engage meaningfully as a couple or as parents?

We stay in touch with the special needs of their children. Are there mental or physical health problems that need monitoring? How are the kids doing in school? What will they need to prepare them for college or special training after high school?

This deep involvement we have in the home lives of our people probably sends up warning flares in the minds of managers and employees in other organizations. What about privacy issues? Is it really the business of workplace leaders to pry into the lives of their people away from the office?

The invasion of privacy question goes to the heart of what it means to be involved in an organization that honors transcendent purpose and encourages a caring community. These are the kinds of organizations all humans seek. And if they really are aligned with a higher purpose and operated as collaborations, these aren't the kinds of environments in which invasions take place.

Invasion implies forced entry. A person's privacy is invaded when they're forced to expose vulnerabilities that put them at risk of exploitation. We think it's the obligation of leaders to establish a listening environment that takes away that risk. It has to be an atmosphere of trust, a trust consistently validated by the way managers handle what they hear.

Managers have to demonstrate that the information they gain through sincere give-and-take communication will help individuals accomplish personal goals as well as increase their on-the-job productivity—that, in fact, the organization assumes the two sets of goals to be entwined. When officers tell us they'd be uncomfortable being reassigned until their children finish a special program, we'd be foolish not to take that into consideration. If a husband and wife are struggling with the competing demands of their careers and family life, we'd be insensitive if we didn't find some way to help them. Those kinds of concerns are bound to affect those officers' relationships with others. They are performance issues as well as needs we're obligated to address as caring colleagues. But we'd never know about such factors if our people held back for fear they'd be ignored—or worse, penalized for their vulnerabilities. We have to prove over and over that our way of looking at the world, as members of God's family and collaborators in his work, informs our relationships with everyone in the organization, from the neediest client to the command staff at national headquarters.

How far do we take this sense of community? As far as we can. At the territorial level, we now have programs that reach out to former officers who left the Army because of some personal problem or because they sought an opportunity they saw as unavailable when they were in uniform. The effort is to stay in touch, to let these individuals know we consider them part of the family and that we invite their continued fellowship in our congregations wherever they live.

Some of these folks may have moved past that point in their lives where they or Army leaders decided they'd be better off outside the Army structure. Maybe they've overcome a psychological problem or they've received new training or education. If it seems in their best interests and in the best interests of our mission, we'll look for a way to get them back in uniform.

The concept of an organization as a family may sound old-fashioned, especially in an age of "free-agent" knowledge workers bounding from one project to another. But we think the perspectives of such workers are often misrepresented. A yearning for more control over how your talents are used doesn't mean you want to disconnect from purpose or people. In fact, from what we can observe in the continuing development of the "new economy," the universal human needs to do meaningful work and to join with others in common purpose are simply spawning new organizations—new companies and new teams and divisions within existing companies—as opposed to creating a class of exiles. In general, people don't want to be free of organizations. They just want better, more responsive ones.

A significant portion of our officer cadets—a third to a half of most classes—is made up of sons and daughters of Army officers. Which we take as an indication that the nurturing, supportive environment we try to build within the officer corps is not only a good atmosphere for growing up, it's also a powerful recruiting incentive.

As anyone can attest who's been part of an organization that assumed its people to be an extended family, there are spectacular bottom-line benefits both to individuals and to group performance when there's mutual trust. The problem comes when employees suspect that they're the ones expected to do all the trusting, that what managers are really listening for is information that will ultimately be used to manipulate them. Such trust violations are indeed invasions of privacy, and workers have every right to build barriers to protect themselves.

But the forced separation of employees' personal concerns from their professional performance is not a solution. It's a problem. If the impulse to integrate our lives is natural and divinely inspired, as we've argued throughout this book, then attempts to compartmentalize aspirations can only end in frustration. If workers are tempted by the indifference of management—or by attempts to exploit them—to draw rigid boundaries between their hopes and their jobs, they'll do exactly that. Then they'll look beyond the official organizational framework for the responsive network they crave, whether it's to be found in volunteer activities—as Peter Drucker discovered with the frustrated executives in his programs—or with a group of in-house malcontents who'll undermine company performance on company time.

Once you estrange employees in this way, you can't get them back with a quick-fix "listening program," no matter how well intentioned. Every personal inquiry under those circumstances will appear an invasion of privacy. And since you've convinced them that what concerns them and what concerns the organization are two different things, that company goals are threatened by personal "distractions," how can you blame them?

As Captain Roland and other rehabilitation specialists can tell you, being attentive doesn't mean you agree with everything you hear. We don't agree with clients who insist on blaming their addictions on others, for instance. And we don't allow ourselves to be talked into commitments that violate our overall purpose. Saying "no" to what you believe would undermine your mission is a way of proving you're paying attention, whether the demand comes from outside of the organization or from within the family.

When I was a divisional leader, a wealthy supporter of the Army in a small community died. She provided for The Salvation Army in her will but didn't specifically designate how the money was to be directed. If the will had asked that the bequest be applied entirely to some specific Army program or location, we would, of course, have honored that request. That's our policy. But the will, in this case, merely designated The Salvation Army as recipient. It was not restricted.

Under these circumstances, which are fairly typical for bequests to the Army, a high percentage of the money would still go to programs and facilities in the region where the deceased had lived. But the corporate entity at the territorial level manages the funds and applies some of the money to support infrastructure that serves the whole territory. The four officer training colleges get some of their money this way. If we didn't use such gifts to pay those kinds of expenses, they would have to be apportioned among the corps, which would then have to divert operational funds to cover their share of regional expenses. So just about everybody is in agreement that it's a pretty good way to operate, besides being a legal obligation.

In this particular community, however, two powerful members of the local advisory board questioned "losing" any portion of the gift of a donor in their town. They convinced their fellow board members they should be allowed to deposit the entire bequest in a local bank account over which they had control. And our officer there, who had to deal with these influential local folks every day, decided it was easier to go along with their wishes than to risk losing their clout by opposing them.

This had the makings of a public-relations debacle as well as a legal battle if we couldn't convince the board to reverse itself and follow Army procedures. I didn't want to undermine our local officer. But by signing off on this advisory-board decision, he had put himself in an untenable position. The decision couldn't be allowed to stand. So I went to the town with our corporate lawyer and asked the board to convene and reconsider the decision. I talked to each board member individually to make sure they understood both the Army rule that was violated and the principle behind it. They voted again, this time agreeing to transfer the money to the proper corporate account, and we completed the paper work on the spot.

The conflict caused a rift in the board, and we lost a couple of members as a result. But most of the advisors came to see our point of view. I don't think we could have achieved that had the Army not established an atmosphere of trust that made listening to one another possible. The locals could have viewed our insistence on following policy as just another corporate turf battle. But these citizens' association with Army programs gave them insight into the way we do business and undercut whatever suspicions there might have been about our motives. We were all working for the same goals.

For skeptical executives, all this intensive listening may sound like spending a lot of time talking and not enough time acting. It's the bane of many consensus-driven enterprises. So many meetings, so much rehashing, so much respect for everyone's opinion. And it seems as if it takes forever to get anything done. Opportunities pass. Creative people become frustrated and move on. The organization stagnates. Is this what we're advocating?

In The Salvation Army, a sense of urgency is built into most of our operations. People suffer while we take time making decisions. And because our limited resources prevent managers from getting too insulated from front-line action, we all tend to hear a clock ticking. We know all about the discipline of deadlines. One of the priorities of managers in any organization is to establish time frames for performance so that everyone knows not only what's expected of them, but also when they're expected to deliver.

That concept is not at issue in most operations. Following through on the concept may be a huge problem, though, because there can be all sorts of breakdowns in the networks of people needed to produce something. What might be lacking is a *common* sense of urgency, an agreement on realistic production schedules the whole enterprise can commit to. And what blocks such a common agreement is the suspicion that other people in the partnership are not talking and listening in good faith: managers are hiding secret agendas from employees; employees are withholding information from decision-makers.

In that sort of atmosphere, management's sudden offer to listen, perhaps in a giant meeting where employees are encouraged to express themselves directly to top executives, will be viewed with cynicism. It comes too late and only in response to breakdowns that threaten production schedules, profits, and executive bonuses. What employees suspect in those circumstances is that managers, checking their watches during the entire dialogue, just want workers to vent a little, then get back to doing what they were doing, only with renewed enthusiasm for cutting costs and increasing output.

Such a show of inviting dialogue is a bust because it's so clearly a tactic and not a way of looking at relationships between people in the organization. If what they're concerned about is not going to influence decision-makers, why should employees give managers information they can use? And if the dialogue is not headed anywhere useful, why should managers consider it anything more than an exercise to please executives who went to a leadership seminar or hired a consultant?

We believe in listening that's connected with a larger purpose. Like everything else in an organization, it should be undertaken with a mind toward mission. Which is why everything we've said up until this point about connecting with an overarching purpose that involves respect for people as potential partners is so important. If you don't have that advantage going for you, promising to listen more attentively is not going to help you much.

Let's consider a business approach from outside the Army that achieves creative results by committing to inviolate principles and collaborative listening. Architect and planner Andres Duany, a principal in the Duany Plater-Zyberk (DPZ) firm in Miami, is one of the founders of the New Urbanism movement, which seeks to capture in town plans and new developments the best of traditional neighborhood design. Its plans make a point of mixing residential, office, and retail space so that citizens aren't relegated to zones of living, working, and shopping accessed only by car. Pedestrian and bicycle traffic, in fact, is given high priority. And there are designed-in public spaces and parks.

As popular as New Urbanism has been with a growing number of folks, it's also been controversial. It requires a certain amount of rethinking on the part of community leaders, especially in communities where the model for development has been suburban sprawl. New Urbanism requires compactness and building diversity, plopping businesses alongside or below apartments and condos and next to clusters of single-family homes. While this is the pattern of life in older neighborhoods Americans admire in New England and Europe, it's different from the suburban pattern that's developed in the era of the automobile. And in many communities, it requires a whole new plan of action for development or at least the modification of zoning regulations and housing codes designed for suburbia.

So the situation Andres Duany often finds himself in sounds more than a little familiar to us. He is an advocate of the transformation of human communities according to timeless principles. The changes he proposes will require individuals to discipline themselves, to agree to codes of behavior that serve an overarching purpose and that honor their connectiveness, their intrinsic partnerships with others. And the only way for all that to happen is for citizens to reach a consensus to build a certain kind of community.

This could take years of back-and-forth squabbling. But planners such as Duany can help a community shrink the process to a week or so through "charrettes." Charrettes are multi-day gatherings of people who want a say in a potential plan. Everyone's invited, including officials who will make and enforce the rules. And they all get to air their hopes and their gripes. But a sense of urgency is imposed upon them. They must agree that what comes out of the sessions—which Duany prefers to be six to ten days in length—will be a design to act on.

As the group moves through the process, Duany's designers are sketching and refining drawings continually to reflect on paper the direction in which the consensus is moving. By the end, there's a completed design plan and supporting documents (proposed codes, etc.) that reflect the larger community purpose and that establish agreed-upon rules that will make the plan work.

Since charrettes are designed to move a diverse group from suspicion (even cynicism) to consensus in a given amount of time, they make pretty good models of the kinds of listening environments that work for organizations. So we asked Andres Duany to tell us some of the keys to running a successful charrette that executives might apply to their own efforts to build trust and to develop action plans people buy into.

First of all, says Duany, "our charrettes have two stages that are absolutely explicit." In the first stage, he prefers concentrating on ideas. In the second, the focus is on production. "If you are expecting to produce something in the time for creativity," says Duany, "you are, to a certain extent, crushing creativity. On the other hand, if you're trying to produce something and you're still messing around with ideas, you'll never get finished."

The idea discussions, says Duany, must be inclusive. He has an advance team responsible for identifying the groups and the individuals who must be involved if a plan is to succeed. He even makes a special effort to bring in opponents, with the belief that "it's the irritant that makes the pearl." But he's very careful not to allow people to segregate themselves into what he calls "monocultures."

"It was a mistake I made for years," Duany says. "We would say, 'Let's let the environmentalists come in.' Then they would write a list. And then I would have to tell them, 'this is not possible, that's not possible.' And they would get angry. 'What do you mean is not possible?' They assumed because they had told me what they wanted, then it was in the plan."

Better, says Duany, to have contenders meet together, so they can hash out conflicting proposals in the early stages, without turning to the facilitator—or the senior executive in the room—to pronounce judgments that create instant losers in a process that's trying to build consensus. And that leads to another lesson Duany has learned: In the listening stage, the boss is there to support the process, not to join the discussion.

"I think that the most fragile thing in the world is a new idea because it can be killed with silence," says Duany. "If somebody says something, and it is met with silence, it will die. It's that fragile.

"So my role as charrette leader is to attempt to bring these ideas to life—first of all, with the prestige of my support. I say, 'That's a good idea. Let's go try it' [by drawing a preliminary sketch]."

But if you're the best draftsman in the room—or the boss of the company—your influence can displace others' ideas, stifling the creativity you seek before it has a chance to develop. So in those early idea discussions, Duany argues, bosses should keep their own ideas off the table. "Remember," he says, "you're the 800-pound guerilla in that room. And anything you say is unnaturally valued. So you're better off shutting up."

That doesn't mean these idea sessions are invitations for open-ended, unfocused debates. On the contrary. "What I do on the first day of a charrette," says Duany, "is establish a set of principles I believe to be inviolate. And those cannot be messed with. They can't be questioned. We are not building the world out of nothing.

"Now, our principle [in New Urbanism] is: Whatever design you come up with has to be compact, diverse, and connected. For a corporation the principle can be: We have to be profitable at least in the middle term. But I think it is very, very important for the boss to establish the principles, the rules of the game."

And while anybody should have the right to say what they believe, that doesn't mean the group is obligated to value every statement equally. Duany, for instance, doesn't allow factual misstatements to pass unchallenged. If somebody wants to argue that a particular design will complicate traffic or threaten housing values or endanger wildlife, he asks for the evidence.

"I'm always correcting, correcting, correcting," says Duany. "If you don't correct it and let stupid commentary stand, then you lose all the people who think you value their intelligent commentary. You dilute the whole process."

By the same token, Duany points out, you win confidence in the discussion by openly admitting uncomfortable facts. "They love it when they hear someone actually stand up and say in a straightforward way, 'Yes, this idea will damage you.' In fact, in my presentation, I will say, 'I want everyone to know that these six property owners here are being damaged by this plan.'

"They are stunned because they assume everybody is always trying to please everybody else. And when they hear someone be straightforward with them, they are astounded. Often, the person who's going to be most hurt by the idea will say, 'I can talk to this guy, because he understands this will damage my back yard.' And we can have a civil discussion about it."

It works the same way in a company in which a new policy that clearly serves the purpose of the enterprise is nevertheless going to disrupt the lives of those who were good at the old method and were comfortable in their jobs. "What you have to say is this," says Duany. "Here's the principle. And the principle trumps your comfort. It may even trump your job. And you have every right to be against the existence of this scheme. But the principle is right. And this is the right thing for us to do."

There's only one kind of atmosphere in which a statement like that will be seen as anything other than brutal and insulting—an atmosphere in which common, overriding principles are clear to everyone and in which there is candor on all sides of a continuing dialogue. Getting your people to buy into honesty on that level is the payoff for buying into their concerns on every other level. You have to listen to be heard.

A charrette is a compacted form of what should be going on in every organization all the time. What makes so many meetings in so many companies so unproductive is that there's precious little buy-in at the most fundamental levels. People don't know what they're there for. And they don't trust the motives of others in the room. To escape that bind, you have to get general agreement on answers to these two questions: What are the principles we all hold sacred no matter what? How is the purpose of this project connected to those principles?

Duany gets the first question out of the way in day one of a charrette. The second question is the measuring stick he uses for the proposals to follow. Once it's clear that everyone is committed to performance in line with the principles, that there are no hidden agendas, then the listening becomes purposeful and productive. The process accelerates from brainstorming to production. Each discussion can focus on what's likely to work for the common purpose rather than on imagined threats and ulterior motives.

Once a consensus plan emerges, it has imbedded within it the inviolate principles and the commitments of the collaborators, who now become advocates. Given a week of intensive listening to strangers, Duany can plan a whole town this way. So it's not unreasonable to assume that a group of like-minded colleagues can take a little more time and refine a product or service that creates value for customers and pride in performance for workers.

6

SPREAD THE
RESPONSIBILITY,
SHARE THE PROFITS

Let's now talk about ways to streamline your means when you've settled on your ends. All kinds of opportunities open up when you can successfully answer the two questions we offered at the end of the last chapter: What are your inviolate principles? And how does what you're doing or what you intend to do reflect those principles?

Principles shape purpose. If your people share a passion for that purpose, if they see the inherent connection between what they aspire to as meaning-seeking individuals and what the organization holds sacred, then you have a mission to organize around. And suddenly, the way to get from where you are to where you want to be becomes clearer.

You can trust the power of your mission to orient you continually. You can afford a diversity of approaches and even occasional setbacks. You don't have to have all the answers. Because people are clear about the purpose of their work and committed to performing in harmony with that purpose, managing becomes a matter of removing obstacles, especially the obstacles that obscure accountability and opportunity.

Your people must be convinced that failure and success depend largely on them, that they will be held accountable for falling short of agreed-upon goals *and* that they will share in the benefits that come from achieving them. This means you, as the manager, must commit to giving authority to innovate and equity in outcomes to the people you expect to feel connected to organizational goals and responsible for performance.

Spreading responsibility and control in this way sucks some of the air out of traditional hierarchies. It demystifies leadership, particularly the brand of leadership practiced by the CEO as commanding general. But it's an enormous energy saver.

Think of what happens in even the best-run corporations when powerful CEOs retire. Immediately, there's speculation about who will succeed the old boss and who will most certainly have to leave because they were passed over for the top job. Everybody just assumes these highly qualified executives, people who may have trained for years under the retiring CEO and possess all kinds of skills and knowledge the company needs, will have to move on because they lost the inside competition to be Number 1. What a waste of talent! What a distraction from the work of the organization! How do you avoid that? By diminishing the concern with who's Number 1. By keeping the focus on the shared purpose of the organization instead of on the people who for the time being serve as its senior leaders.

It's very unlikely any veteran officer would leave The Salvation Army because he or she felt diminished in stature by "settling" for a subordinate job. The fact is, there aren't a lot of subordinate positions in the Army, even though we all have reporting responsibilities to others throughout our careers. Despite the uniforms, the officer ranks, and the other military trappings, the style we've evolved is more collaborative and horizontal than hierarchal and vertical. And it's not just an attitude we encourage to make junior people comfortable with thankless work. Officers throughout our organization *feel* as if they have important commands, because they *do* have important commands.

By the time senior officers have enough experience behind them to be considered for a territorial or national commander's post, they will have had chances to test their talents in all sorts of positions of responsibility. Many of these officers will have long ago decided that, for them, the greatest rewards are to be found in local and regional assignments they love and are good at. Many aren't interested in headquarters jobs because you don't move up in the Army to get more responsibility. It comes to you from the moment you accept your first post. And you don't need to be in a headquarters assignment to feel the impact of what you do in others' lives. On the contrary, officers in a small or medium-sized city will probably see more people every day who rely directly on them—and let them know it—than the commissioners who command the four U.S. territories and our national headquarters.

Mary West is a good example of that. She's a Salvation Army major in Wooster, Ohio, a town of 12,000 in a county of 100,000. Major West is the first to tell you that she's not gifted in the direction of diplomacy. "I'm not a patient person," she admits. In fact, she's so direct and action-oriented that she'd almost certainly ruffle feathers if she served on a large staff that required sensitive dealings with those she reported to and those who reported to her. But left on her own to build programs and to cultivate community relationships in her own way, Major West is a force to be reckoned with.

She took over in Wooster in 1996 when our center there was $150,000 in debt and struggling for direction. She reorganized the local advisory board, adding seven prominent folks who could make things happen in the community, and launched a $1.45 million fund-raising campaign that, she's proud to say, "cost us only $5,000" in overhead expenses. "I'm a risk taker," she says.

And her risks often pay off. Over five years, she's nearly tripled her paid staff to 17 and expanded the Army's services to include everything from family shelters and free medical clinics to computer labs. In 2000, her people served 20,000 meals and provided 7,000 nights of shelter.

Before Wooster, Major West's six-year assignment was in an area of Harlem in New York where we needed her caring energy. There, she was a single white woman serving as pastor and advocate for a predominately black and Hispanic community. Her successes, she says, have to do with making the best of her strengths "which are also my weaknesses. I never take no for an answer. I hold people accountable." When she needs finesse, she borrows it.

"I know the areas where I have problems," says Major West, "so I surround myself with people who complement my weaknesses. I assign them the tasks." In fact, that's one of Major West's secrets of effectiveness—and one of the lessons for leaders who're willing to give up a little control for a chance to accomplish more in the long haul.

"I have a strong work ethic," she says. "But I won't do anything I can find someone else to do."

Let's acknowledge how hard it is to give up the connection we traditionally make between leadership and control. As a culture, we have great fondness for leaders who appear larger than life, who are like mythic heroes. Charismatic leaders personify the organization. In business, they "re-vision" the company. They shuffle organizational charts, get rid of the "dead wood," and bring on a new set of go-getters in their image. Even when the sweeping changes represent true innovations, however, they are top-down innovations—including, ironically, a visionary leader's announced intention, passed down through attenuating management layers, to harvest ideas from the troops at the bottom of the hierarchy.

When everything is aligned perfectly, when heroic strategies work, these kinds of operations show great efficiency. And success reinforces the super CEO's aura of omnipotence. Yet even when things are good, everybody in the organization sits back to wait for the next vision and for the next set of marching orders from headquarters, instead of developing abilities to adapt and innovate on their own. Inevitably, the boss guesses wrong here and there. The aura of invincibility dissolves, and tremors go through the company. The magic is gone. And pressure is on to get a new hero with a new vision.

William Booth came out of that heroic mold. And his autocratic style pulled The Salvation Army at the turn of the twentieth century in one direction. But our customers' embrace of the Army's double mission to save and to serve—and the effects of that success on grass-roots managers and grass-roots management—pulled it another way, toward flexibility and adaptability.

We've talked already about how new officers opening new corps after new corps advanced the front lines beyond the capacity of headquarters to micro-manage the movement. Except for the spiritual commitment they shared with other Salvationists, these officers were often on their own. They were like Major West. They had to raise money and recruit people. And they had to develop skills to manage budgets, acquire and maintain real estate, recruit and train people, operate an office, and build coalitions with local groups and influential individuals—besides attending to pastoral duties for growing congregations.

In the lexicon of vertical organizations, this was building from the bottom up. But there wasn't much "up." It was mostly "out." If they were to maintain and expand their programs, these officers had to be local entrepreneurs, shaping their approaches according to the needs they found and not just according to duties assigned them. They were connecting faster and more effectively than they were commanding. As a result of all this flexibility, Army corps, from their beginnings in America, had this individualistic, self-sustaining feel. And the officers who ran them took pride in their resourcefulness.

There are probably lots of organizations that begin this way. But then at some point, perhaps when a competitor exposes weaknesses in production or distribution processes, pressure builds to consolidate operations and to clarify top-to-bottom responsibilities in the name of efficiency. Vertical organizations appear to be the most efficient, especially when they're headed by a visionary leader who is able to inspire workers to accomplish miracles. When the path is unclear, command and control is the most tempting fallback strategy. It's a tough habit to break. But since top-heaviness is inherently unstable, it eventually invites some sort of revolt.

What happened in the early part of the twentieth century to The Salvation Army was that lots of veteran Salvationists— including William Booth's daughter, Evangeline, who was the national commander in the United States for 30 years beginning in 1904—got a taste of what it felt like to have a visionary leader in charge of a rigorously top-down operation. And they became increasingly uncomfortable with the set-up, especially if they weren't going to get a chance to be the supreme commander.

William Booth never considered that he didn't have the right to choose his successor. He felt, in fact, it was his duty, in order to ensure the continuing unfolding of his vision and the consistency of Army programs. As early as 1890, the Founder designated his eldest son, Bramwell, to succeed him, even though the change of command wouldn't take place until the general died in 1912.

Bramwell was his father's son in terms of his autocratic leadership style. Yet he lacked the advantages that allowed the elder Booth his excesses. He didn't have the status as First Visionary, nor did he possess William Booth's gifts as an inspiring orator. His claim on absolute authority was lineage. And when it became apparent that Bramwell intended to name his own daughter the next Army general, that was seen, even by many of the most loyal Salvationists, as unacceptable.

As so often happens in a royal family, sibling rivalry played a part in weakening the power of the court. Even while their father was still alive and Bramwell was his chief of staff, tension began building between Evangeline in America and Bramwell in England. Her clout within and outside of the worldwide organization grew along with the expansion of the Army's base in the United States, and it had become all but impossible for Bramwell to order his sister to some new post—as he had done with other siblings—without risking an insurrection of officers who reported to her and without angering American benefactors whom she had attracted to the cause.

When it became clear that Bramwell had no intention of consulting with anyone on matters of succession or of instituting more democratic methods of decision-making, senior officers used the opportunity of Bramwell's health problems and an obscure clause in the Army's organizational documents to call a High Council of officers and replace him in 1929. Evangeline probably thought her fellow officers would elect her to lead them. But weary, at least for the time being, of the Booths, the council instead elevated Edward J. Higgins, Bramwell's chief of staff. Evangeline would have to wait until 1934 for her chance to become general. And by that time, the absolute authority of the office had been broken and the process of decision-making had become more democratized.

By 1931, a Commissioners Conference had instituted three crucial reforms: The responsibility of picking a successor passed from the general to a High Council of electors; a mandatory retirement age would keep a general from ruling for life; and instead of the international commander holding title to assets, a trustee company would have legal possession of all Army property.

That's how the Army came to reverse itself in building a management structure that more closely reflects what it does. We admire and try to instill leadership qualities in our people, but we are not a leader-driven organization. And while we modify our strategies to match the needs of customers, we are not market-driven either. We are *mission-driven*. Our purpose is bigger than any program, any process, any individual officer—including the one who may temporarily occupy the CEO's office.

Instead of inhibiting a leader, such a realization is actually liberating. When you know the entire organization is not waiting with baited breath for your every utterance, you're free to act boldly, as long as what you intend is in line with your transcendent purpose. You can even fail from time to time without the roof caving in. Your partners will be there.

I needed the consolation of that truth when I was appointed national commander by the international general in 1995. When the call came, I was flat on my back, still struggling to recover from back surgery. Just four months before, I had been injured when a house deck collapsed in Atlanta and I fell 20 feet to the ground. My physical rehabilitation was complicated because the injury was so close to my spinal column. Even after weeks of therapy, I was so weak I couldn't sit up in a chair to brush my teeth. How in the world, I thought, am I going to be able to assume the duties of national commander?

Outsiders might have been even more puzzled. The general's decision seemed fraught with risk. The Salvation Army in the United States is a $2 billion-a-year enterprise employing thousands and serving millions. Surely it requires full strength and stamina from the executive charged with "running" it.

But our organizational structure doesn't require any single person to "run" it. Our cause is bigger than any individual. And because we're all moving in the same direction, we can easily lend support to one another. There's always a back-up, always a Plan B. So the general wasn't taking nearly as big a risk as it may have seemed. If my rehabilitation didn't progress to the point where I could handle my duties, someone else would step in. The Army would go on without missing a beat.

As I lay in my bed in the days after the general's call, I reminded myself of the support I could count on throughout the organization. I returned to the office in a wheelchair. But soon I regained full strength and was able to put the energy into my assignment that I had hoped for. I never forgot, though, how it felt to be so vulnerable and dependent upon others at the very moment I was named the Army's chief executive in the United States. It was humbling—and reassuring. And in retrospect, it seems the perfect lesson to take into a job in which you might be tempted to think it's you who'll be standing at the controls. From my years serving in communities and on staffs throughout the Army, I knew that the real action and the real authority are to be found where people are served.

Most Salvation Army programs and projects develop when someone in the community with ties to the Army sees opportunity in a problem. Maybe the homeless situation is getting worse because of some shift in a region's economic base. Or maybe too many kids with nothing to do after school are getting into trouble or seniors without resources have become exiled to homes and isolated from contact.

Our local people put their heads together, consult with

experts in the community, and ask advice from those they know in other Army corps. They come up with an approach, perhaps one that borrows from the best of similar Army programs around the nation. But it's nonetheless tailored to their specific needs. Then, usually in consultation with their local advisory board, they develop a strategy for funding it.

That strategy almost always requires a grass-roots entrepreneurial touch. We're always looking for programs that can become self-sustaining, whether it's a program like the Campus Corner Café service for the homeless in Las Vegas we talked about in Chapter 4 or a project that comes with an endowment attached, such as the San Diego community center made possible by Joan Kroc's gift.

Local financial autonomy is not only preferred, it's expected. There's not the option of turning to the main office for regular financial support because that's not where the principal support lies. We organize ourselves so that staff and financial resources don't have a chance to coagulate at regional and national headquarters. (Remember: in our national headquarters in Northern Virginia, we have less than 100 full-time officers and employees to "oversee" more than 5,000 officers, 43,000 employees, and 3.3 million volunteers nationwide.) Except for a portion of funds allocated for support service from divisional, territorial, and national headquarters, funds raised in a particular community by the local Army team stay in that community. That includes dollars dropped into kettles during our national Christmas fundraising, funds raised by mail, and donations for capital campaigns. The point we made in Chapter 1 about putting money where the needs are bears repeating here: According to our latest reports, 17 percent of Salvation Army operating revenue goes to administrative and fundraising costs. That means 83 cents of each donated dollar goes directly to services to help people.

This means we couldn't run local programs from headquarters even if we wanted to. While we might be able to borrow seed support or leverage transitional funding from surpluses elsewhere, it's always temporary. The responsibility of finding people and money to support their ideas falls almost entirely on the shoulders of local Salvationists.

That burden has not only a disciplining effect, making leaders extremely circumspect about husbanding resources, it's also invigorating. It activates local entrepreneurism and creates pride of ownership. Everybody—officers, employees, and volunteers—has equity.

Of course, somewhere along the line, especially if the plan requires securing a loan or making some major investment, divisional and territorial leaders get involved. We call in specialists in law, real estate, finance, construction, social services, and marketing to provide guidance. And depending upon the project's ambitions and revenue requirements, senior officers will have to sign off on different stages of its development. There is no doubt, however, who "owns" these programs.

It is the responsibility of the local officers, employees, and volunteers to refine a plan that will work and to run it effectively. And it is they who get most of the returns—which include not only the bulk of revenues generated by their ideas, but also returns on their investment in relationships with one another and with people in their communities.

Take, for example, a Tulsa, Oklahoma, program that helps students prepare for the ACT exam required by many college admissions offices. It developed in the usual Salvation Army way. One of our people saw a need and took responsibility for filling it.

Jo Bright is the veteran director of our North Mabee Boys and Girls Clubs, which are located in one of Tulsa's poorest sections. Back in 1993, one of the kids who was a regular at the center was a good enough athlete to win a football scholarship to Oklahoma State University. But he told Bright that he was afraid he'd never pass the ACT.

Trained as an educator, Bright decided to help. But after going to three schools looking for a program that could help her student, she realized she'd have to start her own. So she researched test-preparation techniques, approached local companies for funding, and recruited volunteers to help with the tutoring. In the first year, she had 120 kids sign up. Now, she has over 300 students taking pre-tests, studying with tutors, and attending prep classes—all without cost to the kids and without tapping into the budgets for her other Boys and Girls Club programs.

"We started with athletes," Bright says. "Now we help anybody who comes to us." She estimates some 200 students have passed through the program and into colleges. Some of them, including a few athletes who've gone on to play in the National Football League, return to thank Bright and to encourage the youngsters.

We could never hope to tap the entrepreneurial spirit of people like Jo Bright if we did anything to block not only the opportunity she saw to help but also the opportunity she created for herself and for the community to experience the rewards of their efforts. In every sense, their success is our success as an organization.

Some enterprises are very good at delegating responsibility but not so good at letting those who take responsibility share in the rewards. Often, when local operators score a major hit for a company, the money goes back to the main office, and project leaders who came up with the idea and made it work get promoted out of the territory—or worse, get ignored. That's as cynicism-inducing and productivity-killing as ordering people to perform according to the company script. Why should field units continue to develop creative, revenue-generating ideas when all the money—including the money they need to do their best work at implementing the ideas—leaves the local community? Why should opportunities for advancement and higher salaries require people to abandon jobs they're good at and to move away from people who appreciate them? Why not reward them for staying and multiplying their successes?

By putting so much emphasis on local decision-making, we invite some inefficiencies, at least from the point of view of top-down managers. For one thing, our "product" is not exactly the same in each market. Ask parents and kids in the Tulsa neighborhood where Jo Bright runs her Boys and Girls Clubs or in the Los Angeles community where Irene Lewis's center is, and you'll hear all about recreation programs and clubs. In Portland, Oregon, The Salvation Army has a much-admired program for teen runaways. In Florida, we contract with judicial authorities to supervise offenders' transitions from prison. And on it goes. With more than 9,000 centers of operation in America, we are in at least that many businesses. How do you build a national brand like that?

The question goes to the heart of discussions about what a company's core business is. We think you have to be very careful not to mistake a product, which is a temporary *effect* of an organization's efforts, for its mission, which is the *cause* of what it produces.

Products and processes have to be in line with the organization's mission. Otherwise, it's not operating with integrity and risks losing its identity with customers and employees. But within that alignment with purpose, products change with the times. They can be modified, updated, even discontinued. But mission is anchored in the organization's core values and beliefs, which are timeless and inviolate.

When we say we are here to save and to serve, we mean that as our promise, as what we intend to be held accountable for. All of our programs—our products—grow from that sense of mission, and we measure their success against it. But that doesn't mean we define ourselves by those programs. We are not just in the business of rehabbing addicts or coaching kids' basketball or picking up seniors for community center activities. What we want to be judged on is how we honor the larger promise to share Christ's message of salvation and to serve hurting people without discrimination. Everything else is a temporary means to those ultimate ends. Our mission—that's where our brand-building energy is invested.

The evidence that we are succeeding at that is in surveys like the one we discussed in Chapter 4. The Salvation Army enjoys almost universal name recognition and respect, even when people have a hard time naming our specific programs. This makes us even more comfortable taking more risks with diversity.

Here's another, more practical efficiency issue: There's no doubt that in some cases the Army sacrifices maximum efficiency by supporting redundant operations. Each territory, for instance, maintains its own officer training college. And each manages its own investment funds. Couldn't we save money by consolidating and trimming overlap?

This is something we talk about within the organization all the time. There is such a thing as becoming too horizontal, so decentralized that we operate as independent franchises. We keep having to ask ourselves if some specific aspect of our organization meant to preserve local or regional autonomy handicaps our total effort. The test for this is always what we permanently gain for our mission by allowing overlaps in our investments of people and property. We know from our own history and from the experience of other organizations what it feels like to obey the compulsion toward control. This probably means we're more likely to err on the side of decentralization.

Perhaps there's a distinction to be made between long-term organizational effectiveness and short-term program efficiency. If you measured the success of some of our efforts against the hours invested by officers, employees, and volunteers, you'd think there has to be a way to get similar results from less prodigious effort. Yet the impacts of these programs may be astounding because of the multiplier effects we've discussed earlier in the book. The power of a particular project is not just in its immediate effects on service recipients, on targeted customers. There is also the radiating influence on the people doing the serving, including volunteers who're inspired enough by participation to increase their own investment of time and money and to represent the Army to others. Entire communities can be infected with enthusiasm by the success of one project. And the cumulative effect of many such projects, going on all the time across the nation, is what builds our brand.

If we removed some of the local burdens—fund-raising, say, or budgeting—and assigned them to specialists from headquarters, we'd be building infrastructure away from the front lines, adding to our overhead. And, at the same time, we'd be undercutting local ownership of the programs and diminishing their potential impact. In most cases, that's not an acceptable risk. We'll take the opposite chance, of risking momentary inefficiencies for a shot at a higher return in the long run.

There are more complex and troublesome risks in decentralizing, though. What's to keep these local corps, which are so proud of their entrepreneurial abilities, from innovating themselves into bankruptcy, of over-committing people and money and needing a bailout?

With so much of our financial and staff support spread throughout the regions and into the communities, a resource-draining failure in one place might mean borrowing from others to get through the crisis. Those dedicated officers who assume so many responsibilities could easily promise more than they can deliver. The budgets we're so proud of managing at the local level can be thrown into disarray by inexperienced financial managers or by folks who just can't say "no."

Just as individual successes build the national brand, embarrassing flops can undercut it. We say we're prepared to risk failure. But how do we ensure that our junior partners' stumbles don't throw the whole enterprise off-balance? Fear of that prospect is what, in most organizations, sends up the cry for more control and more heroic rescue missions.

The practical way we cope with this threat is incremental innovation, especially when it means expanding into new territory and committing new resources. We have a set strategy, for instance, for starting new corps. If there are needs we think we can address in a community, we'll begin with a service unit of local volunteers directed by officers and employees in the nearest corps or headquarters. That immediately builds a base of support. We may do a formal survey of needs, perhaps hire an outside consultant. We'll want to know not only what we might be able to do for people in this new community but also their likely receptivity to The Salvation Army.

If the volunteer work shows promise and there's clearly support for more effort, we may establish an Army outpost, with some sort of office or center with a full-time Army officer or employee. One of our newly commissioned officers might be in charge of such an operation. Then, if this outpost develops a strong enough base for Army programs and identifies and organizes a group of supportive volunteers, it may become a full-fledged corps. We commit ourselves one step at a time.

Even with well-thought-out strategies such as these, however, we can never entirely remove the risks of decentralized decision-making. And we don't want to understate the dangers even the most creative and responsive organizations face trying to find the right combination of local autonomy and global reliability. But isn't the real problem about focus, about letting parts of the organization lose not control, but rather the orienting power of shared purpose?

We believe the way to deal with every challenge, every threat to effectiveness is to reaffirm an organization's commitment to transcendent principles. Our advantage—and the advantage other organizations can acquire—is a shared conviction that our purpose is sacred. We're together in the belief that our organization exists *only* to help people realign themselves with God and to serve one another. And we're all in agreement that each of our programs must be measured against that purpose. We're all wearing the same uniform, all working in the same direction. So it's unlikely that any individual or any team is going to get too far from the path without being warned—by colleagues as quickly as senior managers—that they're moving beyond the protection that our purpose affords us.

Like any organization concerned about cultivating future leadership, we have all sorts of training programs to keep officers up-to-date with the latest approaches. But we also spend a great deal of time at retreats and seminars talking about the meaning of our mission, how it relates to our faith and to our responsibilities as Christians and, in the case of our officers, as ordained ministers. So we are not only working on our means all the time, we're also continually refreshing our understanding of our ends, of how our purpose as an organization relates to who we are as individuals.

As long as we all share that mission commitment and as long as we offer ample opportunities to experience its rewards, we can expect a certain amount of tolerance, even from the most independent and creative among our people, for the necessity of oversight. Just as national and regional Army leaders can't feel threatened by a diversity of approaches to programs in local communities, Army leaders in local communities can't allow themselves to feel undermined by questions they get from supervisors about their specific strategies and standards of accountability.

At times, this feels very much like a traditional hierarchy, particularly when headquarters asks for more information about a corps officer's pet project. Yet the model we're really talking about is a network. The Salvation Army is a network of diverse enterprises and cross-talented people linked by a clearly defined purpose.

The advantages of networks over traditional hierarchies have to do with the two-way links that are implicit in their structure. A network won't work unless lines of communication go both ways. You share ideas and concerns with people in your network; they share back, offering inspiration and information. And that information often includes links with other networks that broaden your knowledge base for problem solving.

Every organization tries to link people who do similar things throughout its divisions. Human resources people, for instance, may meet with other human resources people. Tech support folks have tech support seminars. Financial specialists are encouraged to consult with other financial people. And those are valuable ways to pass along expertise and come up with new approaches. But you can't get the real multiplier effects of networks without encouraging more informal, spontaneous linkages that create unanticipated learning paths.

Often this means forming alliances outside your organization. In all of our units, for instance, social service professionals get to know people in government agencies, academic institutions, and other nonprofits. They immediately learn of new opportunities. They get advice on applying for grants, on sources for expert volunteers, and on new laws or regulations that will impact their programs. And they get referrals.

Our Florida corrections program began that way in the mid-1970s when the state withdrew funding for counties to supervise probation of misdemeanor offenders. A judge in the Jacksonville area, aware of our counseling work and impressed by our record of effectiveness, asked us to help. The state legislature passed a law, named after The Salvation Army, to clear legal hurdles for our participation. And once we began working together, more programs grew from the relationships with corrections officials. Now we annually work with some 50,000 offenders in 22 counties, helping with healthy transitions back into communities by providing counseling of all kinds and assistance in job training and placement—all supported, incidentally, by contract payments or fees the offenders themselves pay rather than programming budgets of Army centers in the region.

What's more, the corrections networking is now entering another phase. The Canadian government approached us, asking for help with Canadian citizens in Florida prisons. Although many of the Canadian prisoners, before their convictions, had spent all or most of their lives in the United States, they're deported to Canada once they're released, causing immense adjustment problems. And Canadian officials have asked us to use our experience to help with the transitions.

This networking structure helps fulfill the promise we talked about in Chapter 5, the promise to listen. The only context in which that promise works over the long haul is one in which there's convincing evidence that something's going to come out of what employees say and what management hears. And the only way you can create that context is with a management structure that's flexible, responsive, and trust inspiring.

For managers used to giving orders and monitoring compliance, building and encouraging networks may be an unsettling experience. For the heroically inclined, it might not feel like leading at all. It requires a certain amount of restraint.

When I was national commander, I used informal gatherings and ceremonial occasions at different centers around the country simply to listen to what seemed to concern our frontline people. It wasn't always in the words people used; rather, it was in the passion in their voices when they hit on subjects close to their hearts. That's what I learned to listen for. But I'd never hear it if I didn't stifle the impulse to advise or give orders. If I wanted to make the most of those networking opportunities, I was better off letting junior people pull my opinions out of me. And even then, I tried to couch them in ways that didn't imply orders. Networks respond to catalysts more readily than to deliverers of edicts.

Using the Gallup Organization's years of research into the qualities that make good managers, Marcus Buckingham and Curt Coffman suggest many organizations under-appreciate this catalyst role because they're too focused on celebrating visionary leadership. A manager, by this skewed way of thinking, "is a dependable plodder, while the leader is the sophisticated executive, scanning the horizon, strategizing." And most folks would rather see themselves as the latter rather than the former.

Buckingham and Coffman argue that "the core activities of a manager and a leader are simply different. . . . If companies confuse the two roles by expecting every manager to be a leader, or if they define 'leader' as simply a more advanced form of 'manager,' then the all-important catalyst role will soon be undervalued, poorly understood, and poorly played."

By making too big a deal of the outward-facing gifts of visionary leaders, say Buckingham and Coffman, companies fail to develop the inward-facing capabilities of managers, whose principal responsibilities are not about long-range strategizing. They are about picking the right people for jobs, setting expectations for their performance, then motivating and developing them to take on additional responsibilities.

In a network-style operation, all those functions depend upon the active participation of the employee, especially once the recruiting and hiring phase is over. You can't command expectations or motivation or professional development in employees. You have to conspire with your people to achieve all those things. And when everything is going right, the best tactic is often to get out of the way.

While many top business executives talk about spreading responsibility and opening opportunities throughout their organizations, many find it hard to loosen the reins of control. And no wonder. Chief executives are encouraged by media coverage and compensation packages to think of themselves as heroic commanders. But some of the most effective have led their companies to record performance levels by dividing their commands, by transferring control and responsibility closer to customers.

A great example is Don Fites. Fites is a longtime friend of The Salvation Army. He has been one of our most active and inspiring National Advisory Board members. But business people know him from the reputation he built as chairman and CEO of Caterpillar Inc., the world's largest manufacturer of construction and mining machinery and diesel and commercial gas turbine engines.

Fites held the top job at Caterpillar from 1990 to early 1999. In the first year after becoming CEO, he oversaw a total overhaul of the company's structure, changing it from a classic top-down organization run from central offices to a network of autonomous divisions. "We pushed all the accountability and responsibility down to those levels," says Fites, "creating, in effect, 20 or so little companies, each with its own operational head."

Instead of having objectives and revenue targets imposed on the divisions from above, the divisions—in concert with top company executives—set their own objectives. And it was clear to everyone that they were going to be held accountable for achieving results in line with what they promised and that they would be rewarded in proportion to how they met or exceeded expectations.

The divisions had a lot of leeway in choosing how they were going to get to where they wanted to go. They could choose, for instance, to go outside the company for services Caterpillar usually handled in-house, if that was the way to get the most bang for the buck. That kind of freedom had a double effect on performance. It eliminated excuses from division managers who might have blamed under-performance on others in the company dropping the ball. And it spurred those providing in-house services to create higher value for their work.

"Take legal services," says Fites. "Everyone is always complaining about company lawyers. So we said, 'Fine, go out and buy the services of other lawyers.' It turned out our legal services could do a better job for less money. And our lawyers gained a lot of respect. That was one of the ways the legal people measured their results—by how they satisfied customers within the company."

Fites is a big believer in measurable results. "If you aren't keeping score, you're only practicing" is one of his favorite phrases. So what was Caterpillar's score when he was running things? In the nine years he was CEO, Caterpillar's annual worldwide sales and revenues increased 83 percent to $20.9 billion. Profit leaped seven-fold to $1.5 billion.

When Fites took over, Caterpillar had 61 plants and service centers. When he retired, there were 240. The number of models and configurations for company products increased from 81 to 325. It was the most rapid period of growth in Caterpillar's 75-year history.

This is one of the best demonstrations we know of the advantages you get when you transfer power in return for accountability. No one could accuse Caterpillar and Don Fites of forfeiting the chance for high performance merely to let people feel "empowered." They didn't have to sacrifice anything. In fact, because they made it possible for managers and workers to experience control in line with responsibility, the company and the CEO got record results.

7

ORGANIZE TO IMPROVISE

Coping with change, anticipating change, leading change—these are the big topics in leadership development these days. Anyone can deliver consistent results when you can see for miles ahead. But how about when storms obscure the horizon? You have to learn to adapt to survive. You have to seize the opportunities change presents to thrive.

Modern managers will say they know that the current pace of change demands rethinking old assumptions. They'll agree that strategies built on faith that the future will be like the past are doomed. Yet when it comes to performing with some sort of change perspective in mind, most leaders drag their feet, and most organizations prefer refining old techniques to inventing new ones.

What allows most organizations to put off dealing with new challenges is the gradual rate of change in their environments. When change is incremental, managers, insulated by layers of bureaucracy, can build entire careers without noticing the widening cracks in the structures that comfort them. Wouldn't it be helpful if there were some sort of laboratory of change, where time is compressed and the sense of urgency is accelerated, where the old landmarks are gone and new landscapes demand fresh perspectives and creative responses? Under those circumstances, you could build a model for adaptation and innovation that would sustain you in whatever change environment you faced as a leader or as an organization.

Well, consider the lessons to be learned from this kind of experience: Out of nowhere, a tornado tears across the landscape, uprooting everything in its path. In a matter of minutes, houses are destroyed and landmarks are obliterated. Lives are altered forever.

Long after the life-and-death emergency subsides, another kind of anxiety lingers among survivors. There is a numbing sense of dislocation. Once, people could take for granted physical reference points such as buildings, roads—even the trees in their yards. Those things helped orient them and affirm the continuity of their lives. Then, in a matter of moments, it's all gone. A community, in every sense of the word, evaporates.

That's a scenario that transcends the metaphors most people can imagine for sudden, disruptive change. Yet it describes experiences The Salvation Army confronts all the time. We've been involved in disaster relief since 1900, when Galveston, Texas, was struck by a hurricane that killed 5,000 and the Army tapped a nationwide network to help. Six years later, Evangeline Booth authorized $4 million—an amount that drained the Army's coffers at the time—to help San Franciscans recover and rebuild from an earthquake that all but leveled the city. Since then, helping victims of such disasters has become essential to our identity.

In 1999, the Army in the United States provided assistance to 2.3 million people caught up in disasters, from tornadoes and hurricanes to airplane crashes and acts of human violence that disheartened entire communities. What people need in those conditions is not only help in re-establishing their physical support systems—housing, water, food, power, communications systems—but also aid in reconnecting with something that transcends the trauma. They need new reference points, fresh evidence of their link with God's purpose and with the larger caring community. And because each victim is different, because each is distinguished by losses only they understand, the repair work has to be individualized. The work is one-on-one.

Does this kind of challenge sound familiar? It should. It's a compacted version of the atmosphere we described in the opening chapters of the book—a landscape of alienation, where people feel buffeted by powers beyond their control or understanding. We called it a spiritual crisis, and the term applies here as well. Only the desolate landscape is no longer a metaphor. What we have in disaster relief work is a microcosm of the challenges we face in the culture at large, but speeded up and stressed out.

If ever there were a test for organizing effectively to make a difference in people's lives, in an environment where rapid—even horrific—change undercuts old ways of doing business, then disaster relief would seem to be it. It's a laboratory for adaptability.

Here's what our 100-year experience in the laboratory affirms: The best approach to making a difference in people's lives when the big winds blow is the same one you should be committed to when conditions are calm. We can all still—we must, in fact—find direction in an overarching purpose. And if we keep ourselves pointed in that direction, then it's just a matter of fiddling with our equipment and our tactics to stay on course.

If you're going to be consistently effective in all kinds of conditions, you have to acknowledge two things immediately.

First of all, you have to respect the power of change. Change humbles presumptions. It demands a high price for inattention, for not focusing on what is really happening as opposed to what you wish were going on. It's a reality check.

Also, you have to accept the fact that change is pervasive and therefore unavoidable. What happens during a flood or a tornado may seem like a radical aberration, a tragic interruption of everyday life, but the only things really different about it are the shift in perspective it requires and the sense of urgency it demands.

If we're not paying attention, the cumulative effects of constant, subtle alterations of the environment in which we operate daily can be as devastating as change that arrives in one big gust. So we should make the most of these emergency experiences; because if we can learn how to perform effectively under those circumstances, we're likely to get better at adapting to everyday change.

We tell our people that the only thing they can confidently predict in advance about these disasters is that they will happen. We can't depend on the next hurricane or tornado behaving like the last one. We aren't going to know ahead of time the climate or the season or the terrain of the next big emergency. Nor are we going to have advance information about fundamental characteristics of the next community to be hit. This means we can't plan for the number of people who'll be affected, the kinds of structures that will be left standing, the proximity of functioning medical facilities, the status of roads, the availability of electrical power, or the access to potable water.

In the face of all that uncertainty, in the absence of old boundaries and authorities, some people would have you believe that it's every man or woman for him- or herself. There's a whole body of heroic fiction that glorifies the potential of individual action against all odds. It makes for an exciting movie. But in reality, the folly of going it alone in these kinds of emergencies becomes obvious rather quickly.

Being cut off from a community of support is what makes a disaster a disaster. It's part of the problem, not part of the solution. One or two individuals might escape the consequences of catastrophe by acting entirely on their own. But the preservation of life and property on a meaningful scale depends on concerted effort, on committed people working together.

So here's the fundamental lesson of confronting change: The need to organize is as inescapable as change itself. If our work in disaster relief proves nothing else, it demonstrates that you have to have a plan; that you have to have systems that help you implement that plan under pressure; and that you have to have enough trust in the reason you're there and in the people you're working with to replace the old plan with a new one as soon as conditions demand it.

To get past some of the confusion disasters inspire, it helps, we think, to break them down into components we can deal with. The Salvation Army organizes for three distinct phases of an emergency. Each stage may present different demands and require a different set of skills. But you can count on this cycle applying to all these kinds of events.

First is the response phase. Rescue workers rush in. Field support systems are quickly set up. Everything is concentrated on the effort to save and sustain life.

Often, the best help we can provide in this stage is centered around feeding people, both survivors and rescue workers. In the first hours and days after disaster strikes, one of the most valued gifts we can offer is a hot meal or even just a cup of coffee. And we've developed mobile systems—canteens on wheels and self-supporting field kitchens—to get to emergency sites fast. Within 20 minutes of the explosion of a terrorist bomb at Oklahoma City's federal building in 1995, for instance, we had three canteens on site to serve rescue workers.

The second stage is the recovery stage, when we're past the initial shock of the event and begin to assess damage and pick up the pieces. We maintain our regular meal services and begin helping with stopgap needs, such as clothing, shelter, and living expenses. Months after the floods that devastated the Grand Forks, North Dakota, area in 1997, the Army was still serving 3,000 meals a day to workers and survivors.

In some places, we'll act as a kind of hub for others' efforts. In Texas, for instance, the state has designated us as the official coordinator for all private disaster relief.

The final stage is the restoration and rebuilding phase, which could go on for months, even years, after the event. Once the debris is cleared and transitional needs are met, it's time to think about what comes next, about reassembling the fragments and creating a foundation for the future.

If you ask most people what you have to do in crisis situations, they would probably focus on just the first phase, rescue. And, certainly, that's where the initial energy and resources are invested. But if you plotted the effects of disasters on a timeline, the period in which rescue and immediate relief are the concerns is relatively short. Most of the effects, especially the emotional impacts of the experience, are spread out in a prolonged aftermath. And what's necessary in that period has less to do with heroic responses than with reliable support and effective networking with other organizations and government agencies.

Let's take, for example, the wide path of destruction Hurricane Floyd created on the Mid-Atlantic coast in September of 1999. Salvation Army relief workers helped some 18,000 people in the first 12 hours of the storm. But that was only the beginning. Unlike most hurricanes that are concentrated for brief periods in coastal towns, Floyd kept on changing the landscape long after the winds had quieted.

For more than two months, rivers overflowed their banks, overwhelming farming communities and swelling rivers and water supplies with run-off pollution. Before the end of 1999, The Salvation Army had contributed 200,000 hours toward relief and restoration. And the Army's corps operations within the affected communities can be expected to deal with the trauma of Floyd's aftermath for years to come. Communities must be rebuilt, often quite literally.

In a small community near Newark, New Jersey, Floyd and its aftermath wiped out the homes of low-income families who lacked the resources to fix or rebuild their houses. We put an Army staffer in place to coordinate a local program that used donations, government grant money, and the help of an instructor in a federal housing program to recover some 25 homes for residences. Before the hurricane, we didn't have an Army center in that area, but after working with local folks for more than a year after the storm, we had enough support to establish a new corps there.

Here's a point worth underlining: It's not that The Salvation Army has to rally people around the idea of community reconstruction. As we've discussed several times, there's this powerful impulse in all of us toward reconciliation and reintegration. It persists even when familiar ties are severed. Once they've assured their physical survival, people seek to reconnect and to reorient themselves psychologically and socially. We don't have to convince people that they need to recover and rebuild. They move in that direction as soon as they are able. What they require is a little help.

This is an important lesson for anyone confronting the disorienting effects of rapid change. Total chaos proves to be as illusory as total predictability. The most desperate moments of an emergency will pass, leaving victims and helpers to face the longer-range challenges of recovery and rebuilding. Even a massive disaster relief effort, one that may require all sorts of special techniques and skills, is still principally concerned with helping people reconnect with a larger purpose. We're back to the Big Idea of spiritual connectiveness, the same idea that informs our everyday mission.

This is reassuring, isn't it? You don't have to reinvent your mission to cope with change—not if you've oriented yourself in the right direction to begin with. Change exposes miscalculations. It requires adjustments. But it doesn't cancel the laws of the universe.

What you temporarily own is not who you are. Processes and programs should reflect what an organization stands for, but they are not its purpose. Products and processes come and go. It's the mission that stays. It's the foundation you can build on again and again, no matter how destructive the winds of change are.

Still, because people and organizations are so attached to the stuff they own and the things they do, their first, natural reaction, when the unexpected threatens, is denial. We all resist the unknown. We all fear chaos. So our first instinct is often to attempt to gain control by doing what we've always done, just with more intensity. We work harder.

When tradition-bound enterprises, especially those that have enjoyed success, are challenged by new conditions, their first tactic is often to put pressure on the old business model to be more productive. Managers cut expenses, maybe lay off people, perhaps shelve ambitious long-range goals. They exhort their people to deliver more and to deliver it faster and with fewer resources.

Even if such defensive tactics work in the short term, they are, at best, only temporary survival techniques. If companies survive the initial storm by hunkering down, when they emerge from their hiding places, the world in which they'll have to operate will be different. They've only postponed the challenge.

To make life for managers even tougher in this environment, behaving in the opposite way—over-anticipating and over-reacting—can put organizations in just as much jeopardy. If their eyes are only on the horizon, perpetually watching for approaching disaster, companies can distract themselves from their core businesses and quickly exhaust their resources in panic-driven responses that take off in all directions.

What the situation requires is an approach that's responsive and flexible enough to improvise on an individual level, yet deliberate and comprehensive enough to be broadly effective. Here's how that plays out in a Salvation Army context.

In the first days of an emergency, there is an immediate need for cash. We need to rent or purchase facilities that can be distribution centers for food, clothing, and household items. We need fuel. We need to buy supplies for our mobile canteens and to restock our field kitchens. And as we move into the recovery and rebuilding phases, we'll need money for direct grants to desperate families to carry them over until insurance or other benefits kick in. It's not unheard of for us to commit $250,000 in a single day following a major disaster without knowing precisely where the money will come from.

We try to maintain emergency funds at the territorial levels so that divisions and communities can draw on them for immediate cash. But there's never enough to begin to cover the kinds of expenditures necessary for major relief efforts. And whatever money we borrow from those accounts has to be repaid in order to be ready for the next emergency.

This is a potentially panic-inducing situation for local officers in charge of relief efforts. They've spent their entire careers keeping track of pennies, being held accountable for every item in their budgets. To commit themselves to something as modest as repairing the community center van, they have to know where the money is coming from. Now, they're expected to obligate their operations for amounts that could bankrupt them.

So we have this collision of financial management approaches, both of which are reasonable and reality tested.

The emergency demands high flexibility. The continued existence of the institution requires high levels of accountability.
We have to have it both ways. We can't choose to be flexible and
reckless or to be accountable and unresponsive. So we have to
fuse the approaches. We have to be several different kinds of
organizations at the same time.

In the case of emergency financial management, The
Salvation Army's day-to-day reputation for accountability and
results helps us raise the extra money we need in a crisis. The
appeal goes out, the money comes in. "I've never seen it fail,"
says Major David Dalberg, coordinator of national disaster
services. "I've never been involved in a major operation that the
public at large did not understand and support our efforts."

So we can use our experience in disasters to create the kind
of instant fund-raising and fund-allocation structure that will
get us past concerns that we're overcommitting ourselves. But
to maintain the reputation that attracts the support that backs
our commitment, we have to keep delivering on our promises.
This means we have to keep creating and adapting systems to
get results. That's where the integration of approaches comes in.

While rapidly changing events may require faith-testing
flexibility in many situations, they also demand—at least for a
limited time—a far more rigid command structure than we'd
employ in our day-to-day organization. It is absolutely essential
that people know who's in charge of what during emergencies.

To make sure we fit our operations comfortably with
others during these events, we organize ourselves according to
the Incident Command Model adopted by government agencies and other relief organizations. Even someone totally unfamiliar with The Salvation Army can quickly figure out who in
our operation has responsibilities that correspond to the command model and therefore easily coordinate response efforts.

We have manuals that detail precisely who talks to the
media, who's in charge of supply inventories, who has liaison

duties with other agencies, who leads the volunteers, even who writes the thank-you notes after it's over. When we're fully deployed, the list-making, the job-assigning, the reporting back to senior people never ends. Organization is the antidote to chaos.

Yet while the command model keeps us responsive and consistent in one set of circumstances, another, more entrepreneurial approach may serve us better in another. During the Upper Midwestern floods of 1997, for instance, Major Dalberg brought in Salvation Army people from the Southern Territory who were real-estate specialists. He gave them general guidelines, then sent them off on their own to identify properties to acquire or rent for distribution centers. There wasn't time for superiors to sign off on every facility. We needed those spaces quickly. So Major Dalberg's real-estate experts had the authority to negotiate and make deals entirely on their own, provided the contracts fit within the framework they'd all agreed upon beforehand.

During that same flood relief experience, other Army folks focused on purely horizontal management approaches. They were networkers, looking for ways to enhance our service through relationships with others. One of the most effective link-ups was with Wal-Mart. Regional Wal-Mart executives helped us assess our logistic needs, then sent in 26 of their most experienced warehouse staffers to coach us on organizing and distributing food, clothing, and household items. With their help, we reduced the wait in our distribution centers from two and a half hours to 45 minutes. As a result of that experience, we adopted a Wal-Mart–style warehouse system nationwide for disaster relief efforts.

So we have people working simultaneously in all kinds of organizational structures. They may be operating independently as counselors or information specialists. They may be in crews cleaning up houses, preparing food, or stocking distribution centers. Or they could work in administrative office sections processing forms, keeping track of schedules, and watching the money—pretty much as they would if the business were something far more routine than disaster relief. Entrepreneurs, teams, networks, traditional hierarchies, and any other approach that delivers results. One purpose, lots of approaches. Form follows function.

Let's talk about the practical lessons of operating in this fluid context. Here's an obvious one: Once you know a thing or two about the cycle of response to restoration, about the long-term requirements of the job, it's easier to pick and train leaders. You want them driven by mission, not by adrenalin.

Leaders who focus only on the rescue stage and who enjoy success as rescuers are going to keep looking for opportunities to repeat the experience. They're the ones most likely to aspire to the hero executive role we talked about in the last chapter. They're going to look forward to crises in which they can intervene. This makes them less attentive about conflict-avoidance and about incremental adjustments that help an organization adapt day by day. Some will even create disasters—or at least allow them—in order to rush in at the last minute to save the day.

Most organizations have at least a few managers who operate this way. They have little interest in planning or staff development. They don't spend much time connecting immediate strategies with long-term goals. They put off making decisions about everything from accounting software to vacation schedules. Processes back up behind them like dammed rivers. Then, when the dams burst, they suddenly come alive, rushing about giving orders and rescuing deluged workers in the nick of time. They can be so good at crisis management you sometimes forget they had a lot to do with causing it.

But a *real* crisis is less forgiving. In the situations the Army often finds itself in, procrastination, poor planning, and chaotic execution have immediate and obvious conse-quences—sometimes tragic ones. If you can't co-ordinate as a team to help people in the wake of a tornado or floods, they suffer right in front of your eyes. That's an outcome that's so unappealing, it disciplines the whole organization. No one wants to work with people who need to be heroes more than they need to be catalysts. And leaders who lose the confidence of customers and co-workers don't last long.

In fact, experience teaches us not to wait until an emer-gency proves any suspicions we might have about people who crave the excitement more than the need to serve. We find other places for them.

We have volunteers, for instance, who like to sense they're in the heat of battle all the time. They want to be the first to hear the latest developments on police and firefighter radio frequencies. So we assign them monitoring duties. They are tireless workers, staying up all night to keep track of every movement, every new crisis. As an organization, we can use that kind of information, but only if we keep it in context with our mission responsibilities and our immediate capabilities. If these "rabbit ear" sentries were allowed to direct other people based on their information alone, they would exhaust every resource and frustrate our best people. It would be chaos. Yet many organizations risk that kind of confusion by tolerating, even rewarding, managers who run their people ragged with uncoordinated rescue missions.

We're going to discuss in detail in the next chapter the necessity to act with courage, to take risks. But it's important to talk for a moment here about the obligation to develop ways of doing business that "de-risk" long-range efforts, that relieve the necessity of behaving like a rescuing hero—even when goals are spectacularly ambitious.

Gary Hamel and C.K. Prahalad put it this way: "We find it interesting that many companies equate innovation and growth with risk-taking. Sure calculated risks must be taken, but getting to the future first is not simply a matter of having more risk-takers. Getting to the future first is less about making heroic investments than it is about de-risking heroic ambitions."

The "de-risking" process calls for "using the tools of resource leverage," say Hamel and Prahalad. This means that once you have a larger purpose, a direction in which to point your efforts, then success is going to depend upon your abilities to uncomplicate the organization's progress toward it.

When you understand the life cycle of crises, when you see how relatively short a time anyone's required to be a rescuer, you're much more likely to discipline your efforts to have impacts over the long haul. One good place to put those energies is in refining listening skills.

We devoted a whole chapter to listening as a key component of effective management. But it's an even bigger factor when the pressure is on; because even though the emotional need to talk to someone may be higher in these emergencies, there are fewer available ears. Everyone is in a hurry, caught up in the need to do something, when the most significant, community-building service they could provide would be to slow down and empathize.

This is an unsurpassed resource-leveraging opportunity. When the emergency passes, everyone remembers who was there beside them, listening to them pour their hearts out, even if there was nothing anyone could do at the moment to fix things. "This has become a hallmark activity of the Army," says Major Dalberg.

"If you haven't been through these kinds of experiences, it's hard to understand the losses that are involved. And we're not talking just the physical losses. People are caught up in their grief. They are stunned by their experiences. To be a good listener, to put an arm around a shoulder and empathize—even to cry with them—that's more important than anything else you can do. In these kinds of situations, the Army becomes a listening post for a lot of people."

We don't wait for people who are hurting to come to us. We mobilize our efforts, taking our canteens to sites where rescue workers can take a break for coffee and a sandwich. And where we have the equipment, we create field offices in self-supporting recreational vehicles we drive right into neighborhoods affected by storms or tornadoes. We may maintain those RVs on location for months, becoming part of the fabric of the community-rebuilding process.

If we're true to our commitment and persist, in the face of all sorts of logistical hassles, in providing empathetic service and determined outreach, we find it directly affects our abilities to attract support. Even in crises—no, *especially* in crises—establishing a listening relationship has a bottom-line impact, and not just because of what it offers our customers.

Just as challenges increase in crises, so do feelings of accomplishment and opportunities for outreach. Many of our officers can trace their careers' beginnings to serving as volunteers for disaster relief. Influential citizens become active on our advisory boards because of how they see us work during emergencies. State and local officials who might have resisted the involvement of a private agency before their experience with us become lifelong allies.

We seed the potential for all that good will through cross-training. And we cross-train by necessity. No organization can afford to have a network of specialists and all their equipment hovering in every region waiting for the next disaster. You have to be able to call upon people who have other everyday obligations. Remember our discussion in Chapter 3 about gaining multiplier effects from "converting" people and resources to new purposes? Well, disaster relief calls for conversion in a hurry.

Almost all of the people we rely upon in these emergencies have other jobs, either in the Army, or, if they're volunteers, in the private sector. A crucial—perhaps *the* crucial—aspect of our relief mission is our ability to activate this army within the Army instantly when disaster strikes. When they return to their regular jobs, they're more experienced in adapting quickly under intense pressure to the desperate needs of clients wherever they find them. And they're renewed with the spirit of service.

The impact on volunteers is dramatic. Because of the limited shelter available for rescue workers in floods of 1997 near Grand Forks, North Dakota, we flew in volunteers from other cities, using flights donated by Northwest Airlines. We would bring in as many as 250 volunteers on those flights. Most spent their days in clean-up crews, helping residents haul damaged household goods out of their homes and removing mud and water from floors and walls. Then they would get back on the planes at night in order to return to their own homes.

It was exhausting, emotional work. Every day, the volunteers saw people very much like themselves—people with families, jobs, pets, and treasures accumulated over lifetimes. In a matter of a few hours, the floods had put all those things in jeopardy. And dealing with survivors in such disasters can shatter rescue workers' securities.

Yet the conversation among the volunteers on those Northwest flights home was not about how depressing the experience had been. Just the opposite. They talked about how their own lives had been changed for the better by the opportunity to help.

"You hear that all the time," says Major Dalberg. "I don't know how anyone can go through a major disaster and not be changed by the experience."

That goes for our own career people, too. In the 1993 Midwestern floods, we brought in 250 officers from other areas. Four years later, when flood waters devastated the Grand Forks area, we borrowed 600 officers from outside the immediate region. All of them could go home with lessons to apply and inspiration to motivate them for years to come.

Time and again, officers who may have been committed but not exactly on fire for the role they were playing in a particular assignment emerge from disaster duty with an awakened ambition. They may not have known what they were capable of. Nor, it has to be said, did the senior officers to whom they reported. Having the chance to make such a dramatic difference under such stressful conditions changed their attitudes—and probably their careers.

For a long while, the Army harvested these kinds of bonuses without making any special effort to formalize or enhance them. Now, however, we are trying to use the experience of service during disasters as a part of our leadership development training. We want to make the most of the laboratory.

We've found, in fact, that this kind of hands-on opportunity may be a key in recruiting and retaining our best young leaders. And we already know that the Army's performance in the long aftermath, in the restoration and recovery phases of this kind of work, stimulates our growth in the affected regions.

Isn't that interesting? These crises not only test our survival capabilities, as they test the capabilities of all institutions caught up in them, but they also provide some very real opportunities for organizational growth—as long as we perform as we promise.

We think there are lessons for all organizations in our lab experiences. There are the obvious ones: You can't avoid change, so why not have a plan to deal with it?

Apparent chaos, the stage of radical change that is the most frightening, occupies the briefest segment of the crisis time line. So why orient your whole operation to that phase? It's nice to be rescued—even nicer to be the rescuer—but you can't organize for the long haul if you're looking for opportunities for heroism. The aim should be to create an atmosphere that accommodates change without heroes.

Don't let a sense of urgency undermine your best resource-leveraging asset—your commitment to listen attentively to customers and employees. The tougher things get, the higher the value of empathy and the longer the residual effect of moments set aside for hearing others over the din of confusion.

Now, let's consider the more subtle but deeply rooted lesson of the crisis laboratory. What remains unnerving for control freaks, no matter how successfully their operations weather these events, is that there is no management template for coping with or leading change. There's no one way of organizing yourself that will guarantee your survival, let alone your growth. There's nothing to hold onto but purpose.

The purpose that directs you best in emergencies is the same one that orients you in more predictable circumstances. When change forces adaptations, you'll have to revamp strategies, set up multiple structures, rip away layers of bureaucracy. But you must hold sacred and inviolate the core principles we've talked about throughout these pages.

Your efforts must reflect the need to connect with something that transcends the immediate trauma, something bigger and longer lasting than anything a tornado, even a literal tornado, can endanger. And they must promote the integration of individuals into a community of caring. If those ideas aren't honored in some fashion in your mission statement, your vision, your core values, or whatever name you have for your purpose, you shouldn't wait for a crisis to prove your shortsightedness.

What ultimately gives you the hope of influence is not that the world is predictable and controllable and that, therefore, all you need is the right strategy to control it—because we know that's not true. Rather, the hope is in adapting to constantly changing events in ways that keep you aligned with unchanging, overarching principles.

Faith in purpose and trust in others who, like you, have committed to acting in accord with that purpose are what are rewarded when radical change threatens an organization. This suggests how well the same principles serve you when times are not nearly so tough.

If we were looking for the application of some of these ideas in areas far removed from The Salvation Army's focus in disaster relief, why not turn to a field that lends its metaphors to business all the time—the field of sports. And let's pick a sport in which it's clear that strategies are tested against disruptive change continually throughout a game.

American football provides a pretty good context because, with 11 players on each team and with so many defined roles for team-members, the game requires a classic hierarchical management system. And football coaches, by nature, are control freaks. Over the course of their careers, they accumulate nightmarish memories of victories that could have been pulled out *if only* someone hadn't missed an assignment, *if only* someone had seized an opportunity at the right moment. So they're forever strategizing to minimize the variables and forever drilling teams to make each player's role second nature.

Yet, at the same time, coaches must accept the limits of control. Victory often depends on making adjustments in the heat of battle. So they have to prepare themselves and their teams to adapt quickly to sudden change.

Bobby Bowden, head coach of Florida State University's football team, has made a career of blending control and improvisation. Since he took over the program in 1976, Florida State has endured only one losing season. In the 14 years preceding the 2001 season, Bowden's teams had won two national championships and finished in the top five rankings for 14 consecutive seasons, an unrivaled record in the history of big-time college football.

Early on, when Florida State entered many contests as the underdog, Bowden's claim to fame was catching the opposition off guard with trick plays. He never fully abandoned that tactic. But as his program grew to dominance, it lost the advantage of surprise. Nowadays, teams that play FSU circle the game day on their schedule and devote themselves to strategies to score an upset that can build *their* reputations.

So Bowden has the dilemma of leaders of other mature and successful organizations. He has to convince his people continually that the past is no guarantee of the future. He has to recruit and train people to honor a tradition of high standards, but also to anticipate challenges that are likely to appear in some different form than what they've prepared for. His people have to be disciplined enough to stick with their assignments in the midst of noise and confusion. Yet they must also be prepared, when asked, to switch strategies in an instant to respond to new realities.

"People don't realize," says Bowden, "that you may work all week on a game plan, then go out there on Saturday, kick it off, get four plays into the game, and realize the plan's no good. You have to be able to adjust."

And the only way to do that, says Bowden, is to build flexibility into your people and your strategies. If you think that's a challenge for your organization, consider the task facing a college football team like Bobby Bowden's.

As one of the perennial elite in the sport, Florida State can pick its talent from among the best high-school players in the nation. Most of their recruits have been stars, often in multiple sports, since they were children. Teams were built around them. It was up to others—coaches, other players, even parents—to adjust to their style, their preferences.

But when they hit the practice fields at Florida State, these players are surrounded by athletes like themselves. Everyone is a star. Suddenly, they are the ones who'll have to adjust if they're going to compete as a team. "You have to channel their talent," says Bowden, "or else they'll go off in seven different directions."

The system they must submit to is as rigid as any outside of the military. Teams are divided into offensive and defensive units. And then those are broken down into position segments—quarterbacks meet and practice together, and the same goes for linebackers, receivers, running backs, offensive and defensive linemen, and so on. Every skill—blocking, tackling, running pass patterns, throwing, catching, etc.—is broken down into component moves, and the players are drilled endlessly on each move.

Then come the plays, maybe 70 pages of them in the offensive players' books. And each play may have several variations depending on how defenses align themselves. The role of each of the 11 players in each of those plays is choreographed as precisely as if it were a dance performance.

By the time they get to Saturday, the players will have met, watched film, and practiced for some 18 hours. The coaches will have put in three or four times that amount of time plotting and planning. And, as Bowden says, they may set aside most or all of what they prepared if the game begins to unfold in some unexpected way.

Something unexpected is likely because that's the point of the other team's strategy. Unlike a natural disaster, which frustrates best-laid plans because of its random disruptiveness, sports like football invite intentionally disruptive behavior into the mix, which intensifies the potential for confusion. And just as in an emergency, when some people think the way out of confusion lies in individual heroic action, Bowden's stars might be tempted to try to take over a frustrating game, to forsake their assignments and freelance something to save the day.

It falls to Bowden and his assistants to prepare their players to resist that temptation, to keep the improvisation within a team context. How? Partly by practicing adaptation.

"For instance," says Bowden, "we have a scramble plan. Let's say the quarterback goes back to pass, gets chased out of the pocket, and starts scrambling. That means the blocking has broken down, and we're forced out of what we had planned."

But instead of leaving everyone to create options on their own and perhaps risk an interception or a tackle for a loss, there's an automatic plan B. "When the receivers turn around and see what's happening," says Bowden, "they know right where they're supposed to go. The ones who were running deep patterns come back towards the quarterback. The ones who had short patterns go deep. The ones who were running right go left, the ones on the left run right." That gives the quarterback new options and keeps the receivers from improvising into one another's way.

In practices, coaches invent scenarios to inject a game-like sense of urgency. It's third down and 10 yards to go deep in your own territory. It's fourth down on the goal line, with time running out. One play to win or lose the game. Offense, you've got to score. Defense, you've got to stop them.

"Every great coach has a plan for trying to put stress and pressure on a team during practice," says Bowden, "so it's a more familiar experience when it happens in a game." Those practice scenarios are football coaches' crisis labs.

The fundamental challenge for Bowden and his staff, though, cannot be satisfied by drills and back-up plans. It's the same challenge faced by leaders of any organization that must be prepared to adapt quickly to radical change. The coaches need a commitment of hearts and minds to a course that's unclear.

"You can get that commitment," says the coach, "but not before you have faith and trust. We have to sell our players on the idea that what we are doing is good for them as individuals and good for the team as a whole. They have to believe that.

"You can't just stand there and order them to do what you say because you're the coach. That might have been possible years ago, but it isn't now. They want to know why. And you had better be able to show them. You need them to believe and have faith in you and in one another, because you need their trust when it's time to act without having a discussion about it.

"Now trust is something that's getting harder and harder to come by in our society, especially for a lot of these young men who come to us. Many of them are from homes where the father is not around. Many come from impoverished backgrounds where they don't learn much about trusting other people.

"You're not going to get their trust unless they have faith that you're going to do what you say. You can't say one thing and do another.

"Let me tell you something else about trust. You, as the coach, have to show that you trust them, too. I tell my players that I will never lie to them, that they can trust what I say. And I tell them I'll trust them as long as they don't lie to me. So it has to go both ways.

"That's it. If you earn their faith, you get their trust. If you have trust, you can ask for their commitment. And if you have their commitment, you can get a team prepared to face anything that's going to come at them."

8

ACT WITH AUDACITY

On Thanksgiving Day, 1997, during the half-time of the National Football League game between the Dallas Cowboys and the Tennessee Oilers, NBC broadcast a landmark half-time show. It featured country-music superstar Reba McEntire, along with a field of dancers and other entertainers. For ten or so uninterrupted minutes, the performance was beamed out to a national television audience of some 75 million people.

The fact that a national broadcast network was even showing the half-time festivities in Dallas was unusual, because networks, afraid of viewers tuning out halfway through a football game, rarely stick with what the stadium audience is watching when teams leave the field. Major college bowl games and the Super Bowl produce half-time spectaculars that are often televised. But during the regular NFL season, broadcasters often turn to their studio shows and their own on-air stars to hold fans until games resume. To keep a national audience interested, the show in the stadium had better be a good one.

What made this 1997 half-time show even more unusual was its theme. It was a celebration of the work of The Salvation Army and the official national kickoff of our annual Christmas kettle campaign.

In the days just before and after Thanksgiving, local Salvation Army folks place some 20,000 of our familiar kettles on tripods on street corners and in malls across America. By Christmas, dollars dropped into those kettles will have accounted for about five percent of our total annual revenues. But the marketing impact of that campaign, the exposure we get for our brand, counts for far more than the amount of money we collect. For years, the Christmas fund-raising period has been our season of high awareness, when people who may know almost nothing about The Salvation Army take notice of our people and programs.

True to our bottom-up marketing style, though, national awareness of the Army brand, even at Christmastime, has been more of a function of the cumulative effect of all our separate community efforts than a coordinated message from the institution as a whole. Each of those 20,000 kettles represents an individualized pitch for support of the Army in that community.

We always want to anchor the kettle campaign in the communities we serve. But in the mid-1990s, we began looking for ways to boost its impact, something to help us call attention to the broader mission of the Army and to strengthen the brand. We had tried using regional kettle kickoffs to capture more attention. But what we really needed was something more ambitious, something with national appeal.

Network television, with its connection to just about every household in America, is wonderfully pervasive and efficient. You can reach an enormous audience in a single broadcast. But there's an admission price for access to those numbers: Mass-appeal programming. For an organization like ours, this creates an identity problem. Can we remain who we are and yet "sell" our message to millions at once?

If William Booth were alive today, he'd probably have little problem with that question. Booth had a gift for marketing. He believed in beating the drum, figuratively and literally. He encouraged his troops to take the Army into every possible venue. And early Salvationists were as likely to be praying and singing hymns in taverns and on street corners as they were in chapels. They converted everything, from commercial buildings to popular music, to Salvation Army use, continually transforming the secular to the sacred. So we have that tradition of audacity in our veins.

Still, the modern Salvation Army depends a great deal on the support of folks, both inside and outside the organization, who look to us as the standard bearers of a style of compassionate service that is personal and understated. Our work rewards humility and gratitude and teaches us to honor the true source of our success, God's power in people's lives.

So we had a dilemma as we considered the opportunity to put the Army onstage on network television during the half-time of a holiday NFL game. If, on the one hand, we mounted some overly slick half-time show, focusing too much on ourselves, we'd do damage to our reputation for heart-to-heart simplicity. How could we maintain our image as a low-overhead, front lines–focused organization if we mounted a Hollywood-style show that would cost hundreds of thousands of dollars to produce? We might even embarrass our own people, the very folks we were trying to support.

On the other hand, if we offered something too modest, we'd have problems getting broadcasters to carry it, especially if it were preachy. And even if they did air it, we could leave viewers with the impression that we were too out-of-touch to have an impact in contemporary life. That would be the opposite of the message we were trying to get across.

The safest approach was to avoid the challenge. There was no crisis looming in contributions. We were doing just fine with our old approach, enjoying modest single-digit increases in annual kettle collections. Why rush into unfamiliar territory?

Ultimately, we decided to pay more attention to our heritage than to our fears. After all, we know a thing or two about putting on a show. We're an Army full of musicians. We know firsthand the power of a song, the kind of excitement you can generate with an inspired production. And as long as we listened to our hearts and were consistent with our message, we weren't likely to embarrass our supporters or ourselves.

This was one of those occasions in management, too, that required a decision without a lot of hand-wringing throughout the organization. If we had waited for a consensus from everyone on just how to mount such a production, we might still be meeting. Among those we'd have to convince of the worthiness of this opportunity were many of our own people in the field. And the best way to do that was to show them. So this was a decision that came from the national leadership of the Army, backed by the National Advisory Board, then chaired by Steve Reinemund.

Reinemund, since that time, has gone on to become chairman and CEO of Pepsico. In 1997, he was chairman and CEO of the company's Frito-Lay division. And it was Reinemund who took a leadership role in both proposing the idea of the half-time program and in helping us make it happen. This suggests how important our ties are to these national and community leaders who encourage rather than inhibit innovation.

Through Reinemund, we established a relationship with the Dallas Cowboys and team owner Jerry Jones, who helped us line up the production expertise and talent for the half-time show. Pepsico, Frito-Lay, American Express, Wal-Mart, the Cowboys organization, and other corporate friends came through with enough money to keep us from having to dip into operational budgets to pay for it. And when Thanksgiving Day, 1997, arrived, the show went over better than even we had hoped.

Reba McEntire, one of the most popular country singers in the world, dedicated a song—"What If"—to the Army and premiered it on the broadcast. The supporting music, the dancers, every aspect of the production signaled show business professionalism but, at the same time, complemented our message of caring. We even had Cowboys players dropping the first symbolic dollars in a kettle to launch the Christmas campaign.

Our people around the country loved it. Officers, employees, and volunteers who spend so much of their time with Christmas campaigns across the country saw their work celebrated on a national television program. And it instantly built pride and rewarded their identity with the Army.

There were other bonuses: The experience was powerful enough for the Cowboys for them to commit to doing it every year, provided a suitable deal could be made with the television network airing the game. Jerry Jones joined our National Advisory Board.

And the bottom line for the kettle campaign? Our collections had been growing at a rate of about three percent a year in the first half of the 1990s. In 1997, they shot up by 15 percent, the most dramatic rise in memory. Some communities especially good at creating local tie-ins with the nationally televised kickoff enjoyed 100-percent-plus increases over their previous year's collections.

The Cowboys have helped us stage the kettle kickoff at half-times of their Thanksgiving Day games every year since 1997. From that debut year through the 1999 Christmas season, our holiday collections have increased by more than 50 percent.

Deciding to go on national television to promote our most visible fund-raising campaign seems like an obvious move now. But we had never attempted anything like that. And while we are proud of the aggressive ways in which we've advanced our purpose since our founding, we are as vulnerable as any institution—especially ones that have achieved success—in avoiding unfamiliar paths. As payrolls and capital assets and revenues increase, so do the perceived risks of trying something new. Inertia builds. And if they're not careful, leaders become increasingly insulated from the need to make bold decisions. But the best ones seek out those opportunities.

We talked to H. Ross Perot about courageous decision-making, an appropriate topic for him given his private rescue mission into Iran in 1979 to free two of his employees held hostage. How do you know the difference, we asked him, between recklessness and courage? How do you decide ahead of time the conditions under which you'll take major risks for a difficult-to-attain goal?

"I'm not sure," he told us. "If you looked at the odds on that one [the '79 rescue mission], you probably shouldn't do it.

"Let me tell you what my mother said when I was getting ready to go to Iran. She was dying of cancer, and there was a good chance I would never see her again because I might get retained over there. I talked to her about it, and she said, 'Son, those are your men. You sent them over there. They didn't do anything wrong. And it's your responsibility to get them out.' And that pretty well summed it up."

In other words, what seemed to many outsiders as an heroic mission beyond the call of duty was to Perot an extension of duty to the community of people in his company. He had to try it if he and the company were to continue to be who they said they were.

That, of course, understates the physical courage required by Perot and his team. Not many business leaders will ever be called upon to risk themselves in quite that way. Yet Perot's reasoning suggests a good way to look at tough decision-making:

You have to be prepared to act boldly to preserve your purpose and to further your cause.

How does this fit with last chapter's discussion about "derisking" the future? After spending all that time arguing about eliminating the requirements for heroes, are we going to contradict ourselves now by celebrating heroic acts?

Not exactly. What we're talking about here is the willingness to make choices consistent with your purpose, even when it seems safer to do nothing. And it almost always seems safer to do nothing. In an environment in which there is no obvious, short-term penalty for indecisiveness—where, perhaps, indecisiveness is even rewarded—making choices is an act of audacity.

In the disaster laboratory, where a crisis supplies the sense of urgency, the do-nothing option vanishes. But in the everyday operations of most organizations, the pressure moves in the opposite direction: "Don't rock the boat."

There's good reason for this. When organizations turn processes into routines, they can realize efficiencies that boost results. If all else remains equal, the more efficient the routines, the better the results and the higher the profits. So doing things the same way day in and day out feels like the right way to be productive. It's the "scientific" model of management that helped make the Industrial Revolution and continues in one form or another in most organizations today: You achieve productivity from uniformity. The more predictable the supply and the quality of the raw materials—the stuff from the outside—the easier it is to squeeze efficiencies out of the system on the inside. Control the variables, and you can lower costs and increase output—which translates to higher profits.

The problem, of course, is controlling the outside variables. You just can't count on the world to accommodate the model. It has to be the other way around. The model has to conform to a changing reality. A business environment may not change as quickly as the skies during a hurricane or a tornado, but it's always shifting, always producing fresh challenges and opportunities. And as we've pointed out in the last chapter, in the long run, those incremental shifts are as likely to dramatically influence an organization as a sudden storm, especially if managers wait too long to adapt.

In too many cases, even when contrary evidence penetrates an organization's internal filters, even when results begin a downward drift, inertia persists. Change is too unsettling to contemplate, let alone choose. Managers don't want to rock the boat.

You can trace many of the lapses in change adaptation to either or both of two excuses. Managers want to hold off making a decision until "all the data's in." And they're waiting for a signal from "the guys upstairs." Both are connected to the most fundamental problem in decision-making: the refusal to take responsibility.

Stephen Covey makes *proactivity* the first of his "seven habits of highly effective people." The word, says Covey, "means more than merely taking initiative. It means that as human beings, we are responsible for our own lives. . . . We have the initiative and the responsibility to make things happen."

We are, by nature, proactive, says Covey. "If our lives are a function of conditioning and conditions, it is because we have, by conscious decision or by default, chosen to empower those things to control us." That's what managers allow to happen when they wait to get "all the data in." They are empowering other things to control them. All the data will never be in. You can run a thousand computer simulations and survey a million customers, but the conditions are never going to tell you exactly what to do. No matter how much we wish it to be otherwise, we humans are in charge of interpreting conditions and choosing responses to them. There's no escape from that. We're choosing even when we decide not to choose.

The second big excuse, waiting for smoke signals from the board room or the executive committee, is just as common and just as dangerous. It's a symptom of a dysfunctional hierarchy. If line people don't believe they have the responsibility to respond to customer demands or to deal with changes in their operating environment, then the operation will soon be gripped by paralysis.

We've talked already about the limitations of autocratic organizational models. They conspire against decision-making in that the only way top-down management systems can function efficiently is if the gap between what the front-line people see and what the managers know is very narrow. This is why command-control structures work well on battlefields and during the first-response phase of a disaster when needs are obvious. And it's why those same structures are at a competitive disadvantage just about everywhere else.

In any organization in which participants are out of contact with one another for any length of time, whether it's down the hall or on another continent, there's an unequal distribution of information. So in order to make an informed decision, in order to have some sort of meaningful response to what's happening outside, managers have to have a reliable way to gather, authenticate, and process data coming in. That's self-evident.

But here's something that's not so obvious: The only way to make that information processing system reliable is to keep testing it against reality. And the test starts with making a decision. You choose to *do* something. Then you watch to see if the effects of your choice are what you intended. And you keep fine-tuning your information processing and your responses to stay on target.

Gary Hamel uses a similar metaphor when he talks about taking shots at new opportunities. "In the age of revolution," he says, "every company must become an opportunity-seeking missile—where the guidance system homes in on what is possible, not on what has already been accomplished."

If you don't make decisions, though, if you don't aim and shoot at something from time to time, you're sabotaging your guidance system. If you don't test them, you can't know if your perceptions are accurate or if the responses you're considering home in on the target or take you off course. You're deaf and blind to reality.

That means we're coming to a conclusion here that will frighten many careful managers: Sometimes—maybe often— it's better to make a bad decision than no decision.

"No matter how smart you are, it's impossible to have a 100% hit-rate with decisions," write Jim Collins and William Lazier. "A good number of your decisions will be sub-optimal; that's just the nature of life. If you wait until you're absolutely sure before making a choice, you'll most certainly bog down in a quagmire of indecision."

Organizations that are run strictly according to a command-control model—including the majority that disguise real chains of command with touchy-feely retreats or shows of consensus-gathering—*train* indecisiveness and irresponsibility into their systems. In these kinds of organizations, no matter what the employee handbook says, everyone really knows how decisions get made. The boss and his or her surrogates have to okay everything. That makes everyone below the CEO more accountable for obedience than results.

To keep themselves in the good graces of supervisors, employees avoid noticing things that require choices they're not authorized to make. Managers avoid decisions they'll be held responsible for but for which they have little support for implementing. Indecisiveness thus becomes not only permissible but obligatory. And the same goes for irresponsibility. Why should employees think anything but "It's not my job" when they don't have authority to do anything but what they're told?

When we made the decision back in 1997 to produce that first network television kettle kickoff, weren't we imposing the will of headquarters on the troops? If avoiding autocratic management styles is so important, why was that decision so exemplary?

We offered in the last chapter arguments for a multi-structural approach to getting things done. A company, especially one with several divisions and diverse products, has to be comfortable with several styles—vertical command-control, horizontal networking, entrepreneurial free agents. And leaders have to be good at moving comfortably between structural models, adapting the role that's best tuned to the demands of the situation.

It inhibits the whole organization for the CEO to stay locked full-time into an authoritarian style. But there are going to be circumstances in which an order directly from the boss is the most efficient way to keep the organization moving in a purposeful direction. If nothing else, it sends a signal to the troops about expectations. Our decision on the Thanksgiving Day TV production falls under that category. The success of the choice was going to depend on how the show went over not only with the national television audience but also with our own people. The fact that we were shooting for an after-the-fact buy-in from our own organization says something about our belief in the limitations of autocracy.

We knew we couldn't order our people to be comfortable with a marketing approach that might seem foreign to them. But we saw a narrow window of opportunity to prove to them that it would work. What allowed us the chance to try it was the bond of trust we have with one another. Our management system depends upon the collective assumption that we're all working together for one transcendent purpose and that as long as we're aligned with that purpose, we should have the leeway to try strategies that might fail.

Because we weren't asking them to do anything—at least initially—other than to try to tie in their own campaigns with the national kickoff on TV, we could at least count on territorial and divisional leaders to indulge us in the TV experiment. We got financial help from corporate sponsors to off set production expenses for that first performance. But if we were going to make this a Thanksgiving Day tradition, we were eventually going to have to turn to the territories to kick in money from their own budgets. This would mean moving past indulgence to direct participation. And that would require much more inclusive decision-making.

So this was a case of using a vertical approach—a top-down order—to move in a direction the organization's more horizontal structures would eventually have to approve. If we're going to issue commands from headquarters in The Salvation Army, we'd better be able to prove they're consistent with the organization's purpose. Absent a crisis that requires strict command-control decision-making, we think most leaders in most organizations have the same obligation.

But there are even more basic issues that link the Army's methods of doing business with modern theories of individual and organizational behavior. First of all, in The Salvation Army, we don't merely concur with the idea that all humans are to be held responsible for their own actions, we hold it as central to our theology and to the success of our programs. We believe that people, with the help of God and the support of a compassionate community, can change for the better no matter how desperate their situation. Their circumstances don't have to define them; they can—and should—define themselves.

That's why our programs are not conceived as mere stopgaps to suffering but as processes to support and reward increasing levels of responsibility. We are indeed "venture capitalists" in providing an environment for people to succeed.

Although it's unlikely the word would have occurred to William Booth, it's hard to imagine a leader more *proactive* in his determination to build an organization that recognized not only the responsibility of service recipients to participate in their own redemption, but also the responsibility of a caring community to help them. And while we've explored in detail the drawbacks of Booth's autocratic leadership style, there's no doubt the early Army became "an opportunity-seeking missile" with the Founder as decision-maker.

Were all those decisions winners? Of course not. But even the failures offered the opportunity to refocus and home in on our true mission. Take, for instance, the Army's early experiment with farm colonies.

High on the list of Booth's remedies for the plight of those lost "in darkest England" of Victorian London was a hope to partially reverse the Industrial Revolution's rural-to-urban migration of the poor. Like many of his contemporaries— and more than a few modern-day folks—Booth believed, in the words of Army historian Edward H. McKinley, that "city life was inherently unnatural and corrupting." So Booth envisioned farm colonies both in England and abroad, where substantial numbers of those suffering in crowded poverty in cities could be moved with their families to the country. There, they could be instructed in agricultural skills that would not only make the families self-sustaining, but would also bring a financial boon to the Army at large, since farm surpluses presumably could provide revenue to run other programs.

There was no shortage of popular support for the idea, especially in America, where the Army even had a catchy slogan for farm colonization: "The Landless Man to the Manless Land." City politicians liked the scheme because it promised to relieve the pressure of a growing class of unemployed and ill-housed. And officials in sparsely populated regions saw it as a way to recruit citizens and build an economy. Potential colonists seemed to embrace the idea as well. Applications poured in as soon as the Army announced plans for three American locations—one near Cleveland, one in eastern Colorado, and one near Monterey Bay in California.

In the first five or so years of the twentieth century, when the American farm colonies were "at the height of their moderate and short-lived prosperity," says McKinley, the three communities were home to some 5,000 people on 3,000 total acres. But all three were failures by 1910.

The problems were predictable. There was too little land to support the number of families drawn to it. And it required more work, more money, and more time than anyone imagined to transform inexperienced city workers into self-sustaining family farmers.

The colonies failed, says McKinley, "not out of any lack of zeal for the project [but because] successful farming required skill and experience that the unemployed urban poor, worthy or not, did not possess. The colonies did nothing to relieve the causes of urban poverty, nor did they assist its worst victims."

As a strategy for serving the Army's target customers, then, the farm colony scheme was a flop. But it's important not to confuse its status as a strategy with the overarching purpose it was meant to serve. Our purpose, our mission, was and is to preach the gospel and to help, without discrimination, people who are hurting. For a time, Salvation Army leaders thought that relocating people from cities to farms would be a good strategy. And the organization embraced it with passion. When the strategy turned out to be wrong, they abandoned it and moved on. Our guidance system corrected itself; our mission led elsewhere.

Looking back on the farm colony experiment, we can see it was the kind of bad decision that has good results. First of all, it fit our proactive style. Booth and his people weren't just going to sit back and analyze the causes of urban poverty; they were going to try to *do* something.

What they chose to do tested one of the assumptions of their era, that the urban environment itself was a cause of human suffering. If that was the case, then a way to relieve suffering was to reverse the tide of urbanization. Those early Salvationists "did not confront the fact that urban life on a massive scale was here to stay: to them no merely human system was here to stay," says McKinley. "If it were easier for a man to be saved outside of the crowded city with its evil influences, then removing him from the city, rejuvenating him in the country, and capturing him for Jesus would hasten the day when cities and evil influences would cease altogether. The goal was escape and salvation, not reform."

The failure of the strategy suggested a flaw in the perception. It represented, in fact, a fundamental misunderstanding of the role of the city in the Army's future work. And it was a misunderstanding that had to be fixed if The Salvation Army was to move forward.

The guidance system adjustment began with this inescapable conclusion from the farm colony experiment: Escape was not an answer. "The problems of city poverty had to be solved in the city, or not at all," says McKinley. "Even had a sufficient number of poor families come forward endowed with enough agricultural skill to make a farm colony work, the Army lacked the financial resources to acquire large enough tracts of land to provide for more than a handful of the city poor as yeomen farmers—nor could the local agricultural markets support them."

A big, costly decision that took us down a dead end at the beginning of the twentieth century, then, turned out to be a means of refocusing our strategies so that by the end of that century we came to represent, in Diane Winston's words, an "urban religion." We'll opt for those risk-taking choices every time.

Let's consider what might have happened had our early Army leaders ignored the feedback they were getting from the real world and invested their strength of character in resistance instead of change. That's a kind of courage, too, isn't it? Don't we encourage steadfastness and persistence?

Yes, but steadfastness in the face of contrary evidence goes by another name—bullheadedness. And it's a symptom of organizational lethargy and decay rather than an indication of strength.

We talked in an earlier chapter about Peter Drucker's concept of "organized abandonment," where leaders are encouraged to ask this question: "If we did not do this already, would we, knowing what we now know, go into it?" If the answer is no, then they've got to get going on an exit strategy.

In the case of the farm colonies, the early Army invested money and prestige in the program. It took out loans to get some of the communities started. There were press conferences and media interviews with Army leaders, who made a big deal about how this approach would do wonders for both the urban poor and isolated rural communities. So abandoning the ventures meant taking financial losses and suffering embarrassment, even ridicule.

Given the context of the times, some officials no doubt would have been lauded for pressing on, for devoting more energy and diverting more resources to the colonies. In fact, it was a made-to-order opportunity for a rescue-style manager, someone who needed a crisis to overcome. So it took audacity equivalent to the courage that launched the colonies to admit they were a dead end *and* to keep those failures from dampening enthusiasm for the next bold experiment.

Less than 10 years after the last of the three colonies were shut down or converted to some other use, The Salvation Army was sending young women to the front lines of World War I to minister to American soldiers. That strategy was similarly inspired by our mission and carried with it an even higher risk in the event of failure. Lives were at stake as well as the image of the institution. Yet in the case of the Sallies, an audacious move paid off for decades to come.

Protecting the atmosphere for risk-taking, for trying bold strategies in line with organizational purpose, is one of management's most important responsibilities. Your employees can't fear failure, especially the kind of failure that produces bad results from worthwhile ambitions and honest attempts to realize them. Those are the kinds of mistakes you can use to correct your guidance system.

The mistakes that don't help are the ones from efforts that shouldn't have been attempted in the first place because they're out of line with your principles or the ones that result from half-hearted efforts. If you don't give it your best shot, how will you ever know if the problem had to do with the idea itself or with its execution?

Eliminating bad mistakes that come from inappropriate commitments calls for its own brand of courage. We can't tell you how often someone is knocking on our door at national or territorial headquarters with a scheme for multiplying our investment income. If we only put our money into their stock fund, they tell us, they'll double, triple, or quadruple our investment practically overnight. We should be interested, they argue, because it's a sure way to increase the money we have to help other people. Isn't that perfectly in keeping with our mission?

It isn't if it makes us partners in irresponsible business practices or if it puts our resources at risk for mere financial speculation. We'll take all kinds of chances on people or programs we believe in. But we're not interested in gambling the money people have invested with us with the expectation that it's going to be used to help others. We even look with very conservative eyes upon real-estate speculation that would be an everyday component of many corporations' investment strategies. One major setback on a deal that might seem questionable to our supporters would make us look as if we had been distracted for financial gain from our core business.

Now, The Salvation Army and other religious organizations that offer social services have another challenge that will test our courage. We are apparently heading into a new period in the relationship between faith-based charities and the federal government. President George W. Bush says he wants to increase opportunities for organizations such as ours to receive more federal money for dealing with homelessness, drug addiction, and other social service issues. The Army is already receiving something like $250 million annually in government contracts for similar services. And the prospect of more money for crucial programs is something we have to approach with hope—and with great care.

In our conversations with Peter Drucker, he was specific in his cautions: "I see more and more government money going to non-government, nonprofit agencies to carry out community jobs," he told us. "And there is a very real problem to preserve the identity, the essence of the organization.

"Government as a paymaster is a very corrupting paymaster, because they think that because they're paying the piper, they can call the tunes. So instead of setting goals, they set procedures. And so I think the ability to say no to government money on the one hand, but also to take it without giving up one's own essence, one's own values, one's own commitments—that may become a very difficult balance."

Our experience teaches us that we must be audacious enough in our dealings with potential partners—including government partners—to set lines we will not cross, no matter how much money is at stake. We have to be able to say no and to mean it. We have to be prepared, in fact, to lose money if our mission requires it.

That's already happened in several cases where government agencies or perhaps just a zealous individual in an agency insisted that we purge a program of religious references. We've already talked about how our evangelical style is different from many other denominations, how we are determined to represent our Christian convictions through "living the life" as opposed to wagging our fingers in people's faces. Yet we are an evangelical church. Our officers are ordained ministers. Our twofold mission is to serve others *and* to preach the gospel of Jesus Christ. And we cannot be who we are if we deny our religious orientation—even for the purpose of expanding our services to others. So we've given back grants and bowed out of contract negotiations when it's become clear we're expected to deny our religious perspective.

Other enterprises obviously won't draw the same line we do. But we believe every organization that is determined to connect with something larger than mere material gain will find that it will have to declare some options out of bounds by reason of principle. If there is no line, no strategy or tactic you won't pursue, how can you say you are defined and driven by your purpose? Where is your anchor?

It is natural to avoid that moment when a leader has to say, "Look, this is something we just don't do here, no matter how much money we think we can make at it." It takes enormous courage, especially in highly competitive businesses. It seems so impractical, so unrealistic. But the truth of the matter is that just such a decision may be a defining moment for your organization. It can distinguish you from everyone else in your business and inspire everyone in your operation. What, then, could be more practical and competitive?

Doing what you know in your heart is right is its own reward. But take it from us, acting with purposeful audacity often wins you much more than personal satisfaction. If people can count on you to behave consistently in line with your principles, there's no limit to what you can ask from them.

When people talk about having the courage to take risks in pursuit of some worthy goal, they're drawn to the metaphors of mountain climbing. Stories of pushing for the summit, of persisting through bitter cold and high winds, of overcoming exhaustion and the disabling effects of high altitude, are just too tempting to pass up. Inspirational speakers invite us to visualize ourselves standing at the very top of the world, arms raised in triumph after conquering the mountain.

The funny thing is, though, that most successful real-life mountaineers don't talk that way. The word *conquering* doesn't enter their conversations. They tend to talk about climbing as a principled journey, where success depends not just on standing on the summit, but also on making the trip back to safety with the team intact. They talk about discipline, about the months of training and preparation that de-risk the weeks of exposure on mountain faces. And if they lead others in the high mountains, they often talk about the courage to say "no," to order a turn-around or even an end to the expedition when good judgment argues that persistence would imperil the whole endeavor.

"This is a round-trip business," says Ed Viesturs, perhaps the most successful American mountaineer in history. "We like to say that getting to the top is optional; coming down is the part that's mandatory."

Ed Viesturs acquired his experience over two decades, first on the peaks in the Pacific Northwest, then in Nepal, Tibet, and Pakistan. On track to become the first American and one of only a handful of climbers in history to stand on the summits of the 14 highest mountains in the world, Viesturs has ascended Mt. Everest five times. He was the star of the famous IMAX *Everest* documentary shot in 1996. Twelve climbers died on Everest that season, marking one of the most tragic episodes in Himalayan mountaineering history and providing the story chronicled in Jon Krakauer's bestseller, *Into Thin Air*.

More would have died in the storms that killed the 12 that year had it not been for Viesturs and others in the high mountain camps who put their own Everest plans on hold to help rescue stranded climbers. What he learned in 1996 underlined what Viesturs had already come to believe about courage and caution.

Here's one of his rules: Don't confuse a specific strategy with the overall mission, a momentary stage with the entire time line.

In 1996, when his team held in lower camps on Everest, waiting out the storms, others passed them, determined to persist upward despite the threat of bad weather. Some of the 12 who never got off the mountain made getting to the top their ultimate goal. They accomplished it. But storms overtook them on their way down, when they were weak and exhausted from their desperate push to reach the summit.

As is often the case when it comes time for crucial decisions, the best path wasn't clear on Everest. In retrospect, we might think that conditions demanded that those climbers turn around and sit out the storms. But conditions don't decide anything. Humans do the deciding. They evaluate what they see according to their talent and experience, and they make choices. Nothing relieves them—any of us—from that responsibility.

Viesturs' experience and judgment led him to one choice, to wait. Some of the other climbers took in the same information, evaluated it differently or ignored it altogether, and made other choices. This makes sound judgment—the ability to evaluate incoming information—crucial to employing courage effectively. No one doubted the courage of the climbers who lost their lives on Everest, only their judgment. You hone your judgment by taking the right lessons from your experience.

What complicates that learning process, says Viesturs, is getting away with bad decisions from time to time and assuming you'll always be as fortunate. "In 1992, when I climbed K2," says the mountaineer, "the clouds began catching up with us on summit day. I kept thinking, 'This is not going to be a good day to go down.' But I kept delaying the decision to turn around. And on the way down, it was harrowing. I thought, 'Ed, you've made your last mistake. You're going to die.' "

He got back down safely but resisted the temptation that infects many adventurers. "You think you're invincible," says Viesturs. "But you can't count on the same luck next time. You're supposed to get better and smarter with experience. That was a bad judgment call, and I'll never do it again. It was a successful climb, but I made a big mistake."

Viesturs applies the lessons he's learned to expeditions in which he guides less experienced climbers. In these operations, he, too, is a leader who chooses management structures to fit the circumstances.

His clients pay him $50,000 or more for his services as an expedition planner and mountain guide. The people who have the money, the physical stamina, and the determination to try their hand at Himalayan mountain climbing are not the wall-flower types. "A lot of the people you're leading," says Viesturs, "are very successful people, used to getting their own way. They are stubborn. They have big egos."

He wants them to take part in the planning and have a role in decisions that don't affect the safety of individuals or of the climbing team. So they are, in many ways, co-partners in the venture. But when they're on the mountain and operating in his realm of expertise, there almost always comes a time when he issues orders that must be obeyed.

Peter Drucker says that among the responsibilities of leaders, even in decentralized management structures, are to set standards and "to put on the brakes" when the enterprise threatens to veer off-mission. That's what we do. And that's what Ed Viesturs does.

First, says Viesturs, he might try to get team members to admit their limitations and to take themselves out of harm's way. But when that seems unlikely, "I lay down the law," he says. "If I tell them it's time to turn around, we turn around. That's part of what they pay me for."

9

MAKE JOY COUNT

Do you remember the child's game of "hot and cold"? It's usually played to discover a hidden prize, sometimes with the guest of honor blindfolded. The object is to locate a concealed gift by trial and error. And the gift is imagined to radiate heat. So to help seekers "feel" their way to the source, friends shout out clues as players tentatively test one direction, then another: "You're getting warmer, warmer, red hot!" Or, "You're cold, you're freezing now!" Eventually, guided by the "warmer" responses and correcting away from the "colder" angles, players home in on their targets and earn their prizes.

That's a simple but instructive way to think of basic human strategies for finding fulfillment, for discovering the hidden gifts of life. Even if our vision is obscured, we know we're getting closer or moving farther away according to what our internal temperature gauges are telling us. We instinctively move toward that which warms our hearts, which gives us joy. And we avoid that which leaves us cold.

Of course, we humans have learned to be suspicious of our impulses. Undisciplined, instincts can distract us from the deeper joy we seek and lead us down paths that may cause pain and confusion. We have to perfect our guidance systems so that we avoid mistaking temporary pleasure for the longer-lasting satisfaction we crave. Yet, at the same time, we have to be careful not to err in the other direction, to be so mistrustful of our inner compass that we can never find the gifts joy will lead us to.

The soul-deep satisfaction that comes from working in harmony with spiritual purpose cannot be overestimated as an incentive for high performance. Throughout these pages, we talked about the accomplishments of Salvationists and volunteers who are motivated primarily by exactly this kind of joy. It's why people put themselves on the line in disasters and why they give so freely of their time and resources in their communities. Joy in service is one of The Salvation Army's primary recruiting and retention tools.

Kenneth Hodder is a sixth-generation Salvationist. His father was my immediate predecessor as the Army's national commander. But besides his love of the Lord and the Army, Hodder also had a strong attraction to the law. Out of college, he headed to law school and graduated in 1983. He was on a fast track in corporate law, enjoying his work in a California real-estate practice, when, sitting in his office in 1986, he began thinking about the future—not just the next five or 10 years, but the rest of his life.

He was 29 years old. "I suddenly began realizing where I would be 40 years from that point," he says. "Piles of paper would represent what I did.

"I loved the work, but I was representing clients whose interests were exclusively financial. I just didn't feel I had an impact on their lives, and it seemed to me I could make better use of the skills I had acquired."

So Hodder and his wife decided to apply for officer training school in the Western Territory. Now they're assigned to the Los Angeles area. He's Captain Hodder, General Secretary at that division's headquarters.

"It's given me even greater joy than I expected," he says, "because it opens even more doors. People listen more closely when they know that you represent The Salvation Army." His old legal colleagues were "at first very surprised, then very supportive," says Hodder. "People tell me, 'You are The Salvation Army' to me. That's wonderful. Some of them probably say that thinking that I must be giving up something to do what I do. But I'm having a great time."

The money he's not making doesn't enter his mind, says Hodder. Unlike many of the young lawyers battling their way up in private firms, "I don't stay up late at night worrying about the future. The Army provides for all our basic needs. So we have tremendous freedom to concentrate all our energies into doing whatever a community might need.

"The challenges are enormous. But every day there's something new. Every day I think what great fun it is to be here, to be able to see firsthand how God works in the lives of people."

Even though it's such an obvious part of our human make-up, navigating by joy gets a bad rap because so many people equate it with a lack of seriousness. How can you accomplish worthy goals if you're "distracted" by the need to enjoy your efforts?

We can probably trace this attitude back to the source of so many other misleading concepts of work, the Industrial Revolution. If productivity depends upon behaving as if you were a machine, then no wonder some efficiency experts got the idea you're supposed to drain emotion out of the experience of labor. The idea even spilled over into nonprofit work. This is all supposed to be deadly serious business. Worthwhile results demand pain and sacrifice, right? So if you're enjoying yourself, it must be a sign that you're not putting everything you have into the effort.

The truth, however, is very nearly the opposite. We're not talking about fun as an escape *from* work. We're talking about the fun *of* work, about the deep enjoyment that seems to accompany deep involvement, which, in turn, seems to be connected with high performance.

Musicians, athletes, visual artists, writers, and even factory workers and salespeople all talk about their most creative and productive moments as bringing pure joy, even when the effort is all-consuming—perhaps *especially* when the effort is all-consuming. When they are totally engaged, they say, using every skill they can muster and all the energy they can summon, time stands still. They feel in total harmony with their surroundings, immersed in the flow.

Flow, in fact, is the athletes' and artists' term that's been adapted by psychologists such as Mihaly Csikszentmihalyi to describe this state of productive transcendence. "Paradoxically," says Csikszentmihalyi, "it is when we act freely, for the sake of the action itself rather than for ulterior motives, that we learn to become more than what we were. When we choose a goal and invest ourselves in it to the limits of our concentration, whatever we do will be enjoyable. And once we have tasted this joy, we will redouble our efforts to taste it again."

Csikszentmihalyi suggests that this level of high satisfaction derives from activities most people would consider high in stress. They are complex tasks that require sophisticated skills; they demand total concentration; and because they offer almost immediate feedback—you sense when you're getting "hotter" and "colder"—there's no ducking accountability. The pressure's always on. Yet instead of feeling stressed out when they're performing in this way, people who report the flow experience talk about how rewarding and renewing it is.

"This is the way self grows," says Csikszentmihalyi, which is why he considers this phenomenon a paradox: Expanding the potential of self depends, at least in part, upon forgetting self, upon becoming immersed in self-less activity.

By now, readers should be aware of the value The Salvation Army puts on acting in line with a purpose that helps us "become more than what we were." And we in the Army can tell if we're getting "warmer," getting closer to alignment with God's purpose for our lives, by the levels of joy we're feeling.

For Salvationists, this joy orientation has a specific, divine source of inspiration. It comes from God and is realized through Jesus Christ. It is not some rare, mystical feeling that comes only in sanctuaries of worship. It is available as a practical and abiding experience wherever we are. It is part of the spiritual connection, the guidance system we've talked so much about. For Salvationists, it brings sacredness to the secular and mission to the mundane. And this kind of joyful influence has a way of quietly but powerfully changing the culture around it.

Joy is contagious and inspiring. When he saw how fellow lawyers reacted to his decision to leave a lucrative private practice and join The Salvation Army, Kenneth Hodder remembers being struck by this realization: "Not only was it my life that was being affected by this decision, it was also a witness to others who may be seeking the same sense of fulfillment in their lives. It encourages them."

That's one reason we're able to leverage service that touches the lives of one in every ten Americans with a core of uniformed managers that represents less than two-tenths of one percent of the population. We invite our officers, lay people, employees, volunteers, and other supporters to spend themselves on behalf of others. And the returns they get from their investments are so satisfying, they come back for more.

Captain Hodder is an example of that. So is Marlene Klotz Collins, a Phoenix TV executive who sits on our national board. "The Army," she says, "gets to the heart of everything I believe in."

Besides her responsibilities as director of community relations for KTVK-TV and her volunteer work with other organizations, Collins sits on the Salvation Army Advisory Boards at both local and national levels. In Phoenix, she oversees our annual Christmas Angel program and has helped build it into one of the most successful in the country.

It's not so hard for most people to imagine that a former addict or convict, someone who bottomed out in hopelessness, would find fulfillment from dedicating themselves to helping others in one of our programs. Many of them lost everything before they reconnected with a higher purpose through the Army. But how about people like Marlene Klotz Collins and the many others who enjoy successful and rewarding careers, who are already meaningfully engaged with their communities? What's in it for them? In a very real sense, many of these people are paying The Salvation Army to experience the joy of service.

They tell us it's not just a matter of "giving something back," as we so often hear. It's a matter of *getting* something back. "I'd much rather be doing this than some hobby or other activity," says Collins. "I don't feel as if I've sacrificed anything."

The core model for joy orientation is, of course, the individual Army officer. In a typical small-to-medium-sized corps, husband and wife Salvation Army captains might split responsibilities overseeing a social services center, a children's daycare center, a seniors activity program, bands and choruses, recreational sports leagues, and ministerial services to nearby hospitals and prisons. They'll direct their own worship services, of course, and meet regularly with their advisory board and with other folks in the community who can help extend the Army's impact. They'll supervise an office staff and plan seasonal projects, such as the kettle campaign and summer camps for children. And they'll work continually to raise money to sustain continuing programs and to launch new ones.

For all this labor, which often starts early and finishes late each day and which provides precious little time off, this couple may draw less than $400 per week (not including Army benefits of housing and transportation). That's after 10 years as officers and includes allowances for two young children, whose concerns also have to be taken into consideration. Fortunately, a Salvation Army corps community center is a haven for kids, with all sorts of sports, music, and character-building programs to get involved with. Still, this kind of exhausting schedule, with its simultaneous demands for broad skills and narrow focus, seems made to order for management burnout. There's always too much to do and too little time and resources. Yet our officers sign on for life and work happily and productively well into their retirement.

How could you possibly compensate people for this kind of effort if you couldn't offer access to soul-deep satisfaction that was intrinsic to the job?

Early on, we suggested that one of the primary objectives of this book was to provide you with ammunition against cynicism. If joy is a byproduct of aligning your processes successfully with an overarching purpose, then cynicism is the byproduct of failure to do that. It's a negative navigation aid.

If cynical attitudes inhibit your ability to be productive, to have an impact in your marketplace, then the change of perspective you need may require you to change your methods of doing business. We've talked about the things you have to do to get some of the advantages The Salvation Army enjoys: Embrace the spirit, put people in your purpose, embody the brand, listen attentively, involve others in decision-making, organize to improvise, and act boldly. But the same obligations can be viewed from the opposite direction, as things you have to stop doing.

Stop blocking access to spiritual connectedness; end the hypocrisy of methods that violate your principles; tear down communication barriers; devolve autocracy; stop being intimidated by change; and quit letting fear structure decision-making. If you eliminate those barriers, you increase the likelihood of your people's deep involvement in your organization's purpose and you expand opportunities for them to experience deep satisfaction in their work.

The good news is that humans naturally value experiences that deliver this deep sense of involvement and enjoyment, so you don't have to train your people to respond to joy. What you have to do is structure your operations in such a way as to not only permit such experiences but to actively encourage them.

If we were to pick one attribute of our operation that seems to encompass the principles we've talked about in the other chapters and that frees up opportunities to feel deep satisfaction, it would be *leanness*.

Because it prevents bureaucratic layering and increases transparency, leanness forces hands-on responsibility for your product and your image. When you're operating close to the bone, you're going to see pretty quickly what works and what doesn't work. So will everyone else—which means there's no advantage to lying. There's no place to hide.

Leanness inspires innovation. You can't afford not to listen to people inside and outside the organization, because you're always looking for ways to get more out of less, always searching for multiplier effects. You can't waste talent or resources.

Leanness inoculates you against fear, too. Fear is no big deal when you're familiar with the feeling of operating on the edge, when you're always aware you can go out of business if you make foolish choices. Risk is not an aberration in a lean organization. It's taken for granted.

Unfortunately, in lots of business conversation, leanness has become associated with heartlessness—as in "lean and mean." Better to be "lean and meaningful," especially if the meaning is heartfelt and soul-deep. In essence, what leanness does for an organization is remove the stuff that interferes with directly sensing the processes that make it work. You sense the reactions of customers immediately and hear, just as quickly, the suggestions of your people for fixing problems and enhancing services. Your guidance system is near zero-tolerance. You are connected to everything. And while it might take every bit of your concentration and energy to stay connected, when something works as you promised, when you have an impact in line with your purpose, the satisfaction transcends the effort and leaves you wanting nothing more than to repeat the experience. Joy in performance makes achievement addictive.

The power of this kind of enjoyment hasn't escaped leaders of innovative companies in the for-profit sector. Words like *fun* and *joy*, which were unlikely to be seen in company documents in the "scientific" era of management, show up in modern mission statements. Take, for example, the nine core values and principles Charles Brewer created for his ideal company, which he turned into the working guidelines for MindSpring. Number 4 in Brewer's nine principles: "Work is an important part of life, and it should be fun. Being a good business person does not mean being stuffy and boring."

Or consider this example from Sony's core ideologies, offered by Jim Collins and Jerry Porras in *Built to Last:* "To experience the sheer joy that comes from the advancement, application, and innovation of technology that benefits the general public."

Or this from the core values of H. Ross Perot's Perot Systems Corporation: "And finally, while we are building this great company—have fun!"

One of the ways Ross Perot knew things were going right with EDS, the company he eventually sold to General Motors, was the dedication he was getting from people who no longer needed the money. "I had computer operators who were multi-millionaires because they could get stock options," says Perot. "And the interesting thing is, they continued to work until they were 65, even though they didn't have to."

When he and his wife, Margot, "would go out at night, we'd stop by the computer center on the way home," he says. "I enjoyed doing it, and it meant a lot to the guys working second and third shifts that we came by to see them. We just dropped in to visit.

"On more than one occasion, one of these fellows who had done so well in stock and didn't have to work at all, said: 'You wonder why we're still working?'

"And I said, 'Sure, why are you?'

"He said, 'Because it's just so much fun. There are so many great people here.' "

This kind of compensation, joy in the work itself, is likely to play a larger and larger role in the organization of the future. Right now, the shock of the collapse of many Internet-based companies is still spreading through the economy. Many entrepreneurs who had put everything else in their lives on hold while they cobbled together enterprises they could "flip" for astronomical profits saw their dreams dissolve. Engineers and managers tempted away from careers in big corporations by stock options in start-ups watched as paper fortunes disappeared almost overnight.

For a while there, all the excitement leading up to the dot-com crash suggested that technology was not only driving momentous changes, it was creating "virtual" organizations that would dominate the future. The "new economy" would be run by temporary collections of "free agents," perhaps brought together for a single project but essentially unfettered—and unprotected—by organizational structure. Each worker would be "a company of one."

The confidence in some of those visions has been strained by falling markets. Still, this new millennium reality therapy, as severe as it's turned out to be for many new-tech believers, has not changed the fact that times really have changed. Organizations may not entirely give way to individuals passing one another on the way from one project to another, but the future organization will be different. And it will be different because of the effect the free-agent phenomenon is having *within* traditional corporate structures.

Despite the setbacks in the technology sector, there's no evidence that Peter Drucker, who coined the term *knowledge worker* to describe this new kind of employee, was wrong about the effect on organizations of the mobility of the educated work force. In an age in which information, rather than authority, binds members of an organization together, the principal assets of a company are in its workers' heads and hearts. If they go elsewhere for better opportunities—which include better access to deep job satisfaction—company investments walk out the door with them. So, as never before, the productivity of an enterprise is directly dependent upon how workers *feel* about their roles.

But what has been greatly exaggerated in the new economy debate is the eminent demise of institutions staffed by folks who will at least consider working long-term for the same company. Management historian Stuart Crainer cites a Business Strategies forecast that "79.2 percent of all employees will be in full-time permanent jobs in 2005—compared with 83.9 percent in 1986," long before new computer technologies and the Internet liberated free agents. "The revolution has been postponed," says Crainer.

You can infer some of the same conclusions from a poll conducted by *Fast Company* magazine and the Roper Starch

Survey in the last two months of 2000. This poll of 1,000 respondents targeted a population heavily skewed toward new-tech, free-agent thinking—college-educated, employed people from households earning $75,000 a year or more and using America Online's Opinion Place.

As you might suppose, these affluent, web-connected people embraced change and predicted a continued unfolding of a technology-driven revolution in American capitalism. Yet listen to how they responded to the question, "What are the chances that the company you are now employed by will be the same company that you are employed by five years from now?"

More than 70 percent said either "I'm here for the long-term" (34 percent) or "Likely, but who knows?" (37 percent). *Fast Company*'s reading: "At a time when most technology employers lose 20 percent of their professional employees *every* year, just 29 percent of respondents said they expect to leave their employer within the next *five* years. In a world that seems continually chaotic, people are searching for a safe haven."

So we have the intersection of two trends. On the one hand, with the transfer of company assets from tangible property to the knowledge and skills workers bring to projects they believe in, employees have more clout than ever with managers. This is why, Peter Drucker argues, they must be treated as if they're volunteers. "They are paid, to be sure. But knowledge workers have mobility. They own their 'means of production,' which is their knowledge." And they can take it with them to their next job.

On the other hand, even with the options of declaring themselves loyal to no institution other than "a company of one," an overwhelming majority of workers still expects to have full-time roles in organizations. And many more than the rhetoric of revolution leads us to suspect still seek permanent roles. "Even after downsizing, the flurry of demographic time bombs, and talk of Generation X, working life retains a strong element of security," says Crainer.

What seems most likely to happen, then, is that talented people will be willing to invest their skills in organizations but not for the compensation their predecessors settled for. They'll expect more from their work and from their work relationships. And because of the value they bring to enterprises, their demands can't be ignored.

Charles Handy, the former London Business School professor and author, says that what this new environment requires is a new unspoken contract between members of an organization. "The managers," he says, "now become the agents of the members rather than their bosses. They manage because, in a sense, the workers want them to manage. They draw their authority from the people over whom it is to be exercised."

While this makes the job of the manager more difficult, says Handy, it also makes it more legitimate: "It is more legitimate, for instance, for the managers to question what should be the driving purpose of the organization, the strange attraction that will give it meaning. No longer will it be possible to evade the question by maintaining that the sole purpose of the business is to enrich its owners, for there will be no owners, only investors. Clearly the business, any business, needs to reward its investors and to provide for its future, but that has always begged the question: What future? For what and for whom does the organization exist?"

We are now back to where we began. We are back to a search for meaning.

To extract the joy we crave from our efforts as human beings, we need to feel directly the effects of our contributions toward some worthy, transcendent goal—the Big Idea we began talking about in Chapter 1. So we must clear out the clutter, the filtering layers, between what we spend our time doing and what we promise we'll do. But doing away with the interference won't satisfy our need for meaning unless what we're left with after the tidying up is a purpose we're proud of. All that busy work—the bureaucracy building, the hypocrisy, the indecisiveness and fear—can keep us so preoccupied that we don't notice that at the bottom of it all is a goal that's so mundane it can never engage us. Too many people trick themselves into believing that what inhibits their happiness is the extreme difficulty of lofty aspirations, when the truth is, the joy deficit is much more likely to be caused by aiming too low and hitting the mark consistently.

Our experience teaches us that you can be forgiven a great deal for making honest mistakes committed in the act of trying to save the world. But people will lose interest quickly in even above-average efficiency in satisfying low expectations. Where's the joy in that?

We in The Salvation Army have always connected joy in service with music. Some of the first Salvationists attracted audiences for our gospel message with brass bands and choruses. We are still an Army of horn players, drummers, and singers. So we are probably a little more empathetic than most folks when the talk turns to the power of music to deliver a sense of full engagement and soul-deep enjoyment.

Playing in a band has also become a favorite metaphor for modern management theorists because it offers so many opportunities to talk about bringing individual skills together into a team. Let's turn, then, to music for our last example of a Salvation Army–style vision of leadership in organizations outside the Army.

Since the late 1990s, the Bo Thorpe Band has been one of the most commercially successful big bands in North America. Traveling from its base in Nashville, the band has been a mainstay on the grand ball circuit, playing at six presidential inaugural balls—including George W. Bush's in

January of 2001—and at prestigious charity functions in Los Angeles, New York, Atlanta, Houston, and Washington, D.C. The group was a hit before the great swing revival of the 1990s, then became even more popular as a new generation took to the tunes of Benny Goodman, Glenn Miller, and other big band pioneers of the 1940s.

Band founder Bo Thorpe always wanted his band to be more than a nostalgia act, however; so he recruited his musicians from among the top talent in New York, Nashville, and Los Angeles and contracted with music arrangers for a wide variety of music that could entertain demanding patrons of any era and any taste. Most of the 18 or so regulars in the Bo Thorpe Band are music-school–trained musicians who have played everything from classical music to jazz and can deliver, live onstage, an almost perfect performance of a musical score they've never seen before.

Rory Partin sang and played trumpet with the group in the early 1990s, then returned at the end of the decade when Bo Thorpe, because of declining health, was selling the band. Partin put together a deal to buy the group and took it over at the end of 2000. Even with all its commercial success over three decades, the Bo Thorpe Band wouldn't exist unless Thorpe and now Partin could compensate their musicians partially with the pleasure of their own performances.

"I can't pay them enough so that all the guys in the band can make a living doing only this," says Partin. "There are guys in the band with teaching degrees who could have much more dependable incomes doing something else. But they have to find a way to do what they love. And if you're in our business, there are not that many opportunities to do this, to sit down regularly with a group of 18 musicians who can play at this level.

"The feeling of synergy you get when you're up on stage with these guys is incredible. A trumpet player may be up there concentrating on just his part. Then he hears the saxes really starting to swing. That pushes him to step it up to match their energy, which drives those on other instruments to keep it going. And the sound just keeps feeding on itself, building and building.

"You know what it's like when it all comes together? It's like 18 people becoming one living thing. It's like we're this animal, this gazelle running at full speed. Efficient and effortless. Beautiful to watch. I can't begin to tell you the huge joy in that."

Getting this kind of reward justifies the organization of individuals into a band. In fact, it's clear that whatever reward individuals could expect from their own talents is enhanced by their participation in the group. "I think that's a big key," says Partin. "All of us moved to Nashville thinking, maybe in the backs of our minds, we were going to become these big individual stars. But now a lot of us realize that we can't do it on our own. In fact, it's much more exciting to do it with these other guys."

Now that he's the leader, Partin's role is complicated by multiple responsibilities—picking the order of tunes, counting off the beat, conducting the music, plus singing on many of the songs. "It's a ton to think about," he says, "and there are times I really sweat it. It's stressful."

But this is the kind of stress that Csikszentmihalyi, the psychologist, would call conducive to achieving the flow experience. It provides the challenge of complexity for Partin's highly developed skills. And it takes place under conditions that will provide immediate feedback. Partin and the other musicians can hear instantly the gradations between success and failure.

What makes success more likely is the contribution of elements we've talked about in other contexts—inspiration, discipline, and responsiveness. You are inspired toward the goal of experiencing freedom, the sense of endless possibility, of perfect performance. "But you go through all this training so you can be free," says Partin.

Formal music schooling, years of individual practice, years more working through diverse music with other musicians all refine musicians' talents so they're less bound by their limitations. "Some people," says Partin, "a very few, have a natural gift [that allows them to play or write almost instantly at a very sophisticated level]. But most of us need training. We need instruction, and we need to work at it.

"It's like weight lifting. You get stronger by training your muscles to lift heavier and heavier weights. And the stronger you get, the more you're capable of lifting, which makes you even stronger."

There's a limit, though, to the rewards of lifting weights, of practicing, alone. The real leaps in performance capability often come, literally in this case, in concert with and for others. That's where responsiveness comes in.

"You have to listen to what's going on around you," says Partin. Music makes plenty of room for inspired improvisation, for the soloist. But solos work best when they're performed within the context of support of the group. The other musicians imply the structure, the rhythmic and melodic lines of the tune, which serve as soloists' points of departure and return. "But if you have two or more people trying to ad lib at the same time, no matter how talented they are," says Partin, "they'll produce cacophonous noise instead of music."

To get the loping gazelle effect, you have to be tuned into others around you—and to your audience.

The founding leader of the band, Bo Thorpe, built the success of his group on an uncanny ability to anticipate the mood of listeners. Thorpe wasn't a musician himself. He couldn't read his musicians' charts. He just always seemed to know which of the 250 or so tunes in the band's playbook to call next.

For a dance band, it's an irreplaceable skill. "I tried to absorb that from him," says Partin.

Even as he refines his crowd-sensing abilities, Partin has an advantage that Thorpe may never have developed. His training, including formal training in conducting, allows him to respond to the music as a musician—to "play" the band, to help them push beyond the charts in front of them to some more complex and rewarding territory.

Partin remembers the first time this happened for him. It was in January 2001, at the Grove Park Inn in Asheville, North Carolina. It was a concert for big band aficionados, requiring tight sets of familiar music from the swing era. Because they know the music so well, people at a performance like this, says Partin, "won't accept anything that isn't close to CD-perfect." So the pressure was on.

At one point, he says, "my natural self just took over. I started directing the band. I felt free, from all my training, to try all these new things. And the band responded. It became one of those nights where we were just so on.

"Some of the guys came up to me between sets and said, 'Man, this is fun. What you're doing is making all the difference.' And I thought, 'This is what it means to live fully in the moment, in the music.'

"You live and die for those kinds of moments. Once you know what that feels like, you can't not try to do it again, even if it means failing lots of the time. You say to yourself, 'You know, we got it right that time.' And even if it means you're never hired again, you know that's what you have to go for. You'll have to play for free, if that's what it takes to get that feeling again."

Our own experience in music underlines what Partin says and draws this additional connection between the joy of performance and commitment to a larger purpose: you have to play from the heart.

Phil Smith, a fourth-generation Salvationist and principal trumpet player with the New York Philharmonic, puts it this way: "My faith is a relationship with Christ in my heart. And if you've got that song in your heart, it's got to come out. It's part of who I am. I can't help it, I have to talk about it."

In the CNN.com interview in which Smith said that, he talked about the blending of technique and heartfelt emotion that's so necessary to performing at the highest level. "I can sit there and tell you to do this with your mouth, and make sure you blow, and that doesn't translate into anything," says Smith. "First is hearing it in your head; the other part is in your heart—having this innate part of our soul that needs to express itself. Music is not just the black dots on the white paper. It's what happens when those black dots on the white paper go into your heart and come out again."

This act of integration—of blending inspiration and discipline—is not just for Salvationists and trumpet players. It touches a deep need in all of us. When CNN.com presented the long interview with Phil Smith, it invited readers to respond on-line to this question: "How much would you say your spiritual life figures into your career?"

It was an unscientific survey, of course, but the results were revealing. Asked to choose from three alternative answers— "very little"; "somewhat"; and "a lot"—63 percent of those who responded to the poll picked this answer: "A lot. Similar to Phil Smith's experience, I find my work life and my spiritual life to be one, and I think my work can be a testament to my faith."

NOTES

Chapter 1

PAGE

12 *At that precise moment:* "How the Fallen Have Risen," *The Salvation Army War Cry,* June 13, 1998, p. 4; and June 27, 1998, p. 4.

15 *Among the "shattered myths: Built to Last: Successful Habits of Visionary Companies* (HarperBusiness, 1994; paperback, 1997) p. 8 (paperback edition).

15 *Little difference between for-profit visionary companies:* Ibid, p. xix.

15 *Most effective organization:* "Peter Drucker's Picks," *Forbes,* August 11, 1997.

17 *Understates the value of what it contributes:* "Can you top this for cost-effective management?" *Forbes,* April 20, 1998.

19 *Top annual fund-raising rankings:* "Giving More: Charitable Contributions Jump 13 Percent," by David Ho, the Associated Press, October 29, 2000 (*www.abcnews.go.com/sections/us/DailyNews/philanthropy001029.html*).

20 *You have some charitable operations:* Peter Drucker interview with the authors.

28 *Filled with the Spirit:* Don Ross interview with Ben Brown.

Chapter 2

36 *Change of uniforms:* Dorothy McBride interview with Ben Brown.

37 *Blending medicine and the ministry:* "An Ordained Career Move," *Priority* (magazine of The Salvation Army's Eastern Territory), (Spring 2001) pp. 11–14.

42 *Struggle and sink:* General William Booth, *In Darkest England and the Way Out* (Tyler & Company, U.S. edition, 1942), preface.

42 *The natural outcome of Salvationism:* Robert Sandall, *The History of The Salvation Army* (Thomas Nelson and Sons, 1947, 1950, 1955, 1968), Volume 3, p. xi.

49 *We closely resemble the Methodists:* Salvationists—officers and the laity at the core of The Salvation Army church—hold these 11 doctrines of religious faith:

> "We believe that the Scriptures of the Old and New Testaments were given by inspiration of God, and that they only constitute the Divine rule of Christian faith and practice.

> "We believe that there is only one God, who is infinitely perfect, the Creator, Preserver and Governor of all things, and who is the only proper object of religious worship.

> "We believe that there are three persons in the Godhead—the Father, the Son, and the Holy Ghost, undivided in essence and co-equal in power and glory.

> "We believe that in the person of Jesus Christ the Divine and human natures are united, so that He is truly and properly God and truly and properly man.

> "We believe that our first parents were created in a state of innocency, but by their disobedience they lost their purity and happiness, and that in consequence of their fall all men have become sinners, totally depraved, and as such are justly exposed to the wrath of God.

> "We believe that the Lord Jesus Christ has by His suffering and death made an atonement for the whole world so that whosoever will may be saved.

> "We believe that repentance towards God, faith in our Lord Jesus Christ, and regeneration by the Holy Spirit, are necessary to salvation.

> "We believe that we are justified by grace through faith in our Lord Jesus Christ and that he that believeth hath the witness in himself.

"We believe that continuance in a state of salvation depends upon continued obedient faith in Christ.

"We believe that it is the privilege of all believers to be wholly sanctified, and that their whole spirit and soul and body may be preserved blameless unto the coming of our Lord Jesus Christ.

"We believe in the immortality of the soul; in the resurrection of the body; in the general judgment at the end of the world; in the eternal happiness of the righteous; and in the endless punishment of the wicked."

44 *Early Army services described as user-friendly:* Stephen Brook, *God's Army: The Story of The Salvation Army* (Channel 4 Books, Great Britain, 1998), p. 16.

45 *Fast-track executives volunteer in nonprofits:* Peter F. Drucker, *Peter Drucker on the Profession of Management* (Harvard Business Review, 1963), p. 131.

47 *Developing a theatrical ministry:* Carol Jaudes interview with Ben Brown.

48 *Spiritual therapy in concert with medical treatment:* A quick overview of "the faith factor" in healing can be found in *Shopping for Faith: American Religion in the New Millennium* by Richard Cimino and Don Lattin (Jossey-Bass). Included in the authors' round-up is data from a 1996 survey of members of the American Academy of Family Physicians indicating that "a remarkable 99 percent [of those surveyed] think religious faith helps patients respond to treatment" (p. 45).

51 *Red Shield Youth and Community Center:* Irene Lewis interview with Ben Brown.

51 *Most companies are overmanaged:* Gary Hamel and C.K. Prahalad, *Competing for the Future* (Harvard Business School, 1994; 1996 in paperback), p. 142 in paperback edition.

54 *Principles that govern human effectiveness:* Stephen R. Covey, *The 7 Habits of Highly Successful People* (Simon & Schuster, 1989), p. 32.

55 *Values-driven management:* Thomas J. Peters and Robert H. Warterman, Jr. in *In Search of Excellence: Lessons from America's Best-Run Companies* (Warner Books, 1982), p. 280.

55 *Visionary companies:* James C. Collins and Jerry L. Porras, *Built to Last: Successful Habits of Visionary Companies* (HarperBusiness, 1994; paperback, 1997), p. xii.

56 *People stand in line to work there:* "The Man Behind MindSpring," Ben Brown, Georgia edition of *Southern Living,* February, 1999, 30 GL.

Chapter 3

60 *Reciprocate for the incredible help we received:* Kurt Weishaupt interview with the authors and 1990 speech before a Salvation Army audience.

60 *Every organization sells itself as a service provider:* Peter Drucker says, "The organization is above all *social.* It is people. Its purpose must therefore be to make the strengths of people effective and their weaknesses irrelevant." (*The Organization of the Future,* p. 5)

61 *Wall of poverty:* Frederick Coutts, *Bread for My Neighbour: The Social Influence of William Booth* (Hodder and Stoughton, London, 1978), p. 31.

62 *Cholera, smallpox, and other diseases raged:* Ibid., p. 33.

62 *Few parsons had faith in the common man:* Richard Collier, *The General Next to God* (Fontana/Collins, 1965, 1976 paperback), p. 38 in the paperback edition.

62 *The folly of hoping to accomplish anything:* Booth, *In Darkest England and the Way Out,* preface.

64 *The impact it has outside itself:* In the late nineteenth century, when large organizations first arose, says Peter Drucker, "managing the inside was the new challenge. Nobody had ever done it before. But while the assumption that management's domain is the inside of the organization made sense—or at least can be explained—its continuation makes no sense whatever. It is a contradiction of the very function and nature of organization." The fact is, Drucker asserts in one of his "new paradigms" for the profession, management "is the organ to make the institution, whether business, church, university, hospital or a battered women's shelter capable of producing results outside of itself." (*Management Challenges for the 21st Century,* p. 39)

66 *Visiting is almost impossible:* Robert Sandall, *The History of The Salvation Army* (Thomas Nelson and Sons, 1947, 1950, 1955, 1968), vol. 1, p. 79.

66 *These roles are something we assume temporarily:* The Salvation Army's perspective on community is derived in part from "the covenant of social responsibility which was commanded in the Old Testament, established through Jesus Christ, and realized in the calling of his disciples." That's how Col. Phillip D. Needham, chief secretary of The Salvation Army's Western Territory and one our most thoughtful theological writers, put it in a 1984 paper. His words ring true. "From this perspective," wrote Col. Needham, "it is impossible

for social service to be perceived as charitable acts toward less fortunate people. Rather, it is to be understood as concrete steps toward realizing the new reality of social reconciliation which has come in Christ. Social service takes place within the new human family which Christ makes possible. There is no condescension in it. It is based upon the deepest respect for persons as potential members of the household of faith." ("A Contemporary Theology of Social Service: Toward a Reintegration of the Salvationist Mission," presented at the Theology of Social Services Symposium, Catherine Booth Bible College, Winnipeg, Manitoba, May 27, 1984)

66 *Business has deteriorated:* Peter Drucker interview with the authors.

68 *You end up with an action step:* Chris Hogan interview with Ben Brown.

70 *General orders against starvation:* Richard Collier, *The General Next to God*, p. 104.

78 *Traditional Christmastime program:* Maj. Victoria Edmonds interview with Ben Brown.

80 *There isn't any hope for you:* "Behold, all things became new . . . ," *The Salvation Army War Cry*, August 5, 2000, p. 11.

83 *Inspirational management in an unlikely business sector:* Bob Byers interview with the authors.

Chapter 4

87 *A company that is evolving slowly:* Gary Hamel, *Leading the Revolution* (Harvard Business School, 2000), p. 5.

87 *When a customer calls the tune:* Michael Hammer, "The Soul of the New Organization," *The Organization of the Future*, p. 27.

88 *Core values in a visionary company:* Collins and Porras, *Built to Last*, p. 8.

89 *In the dot-com era, trust remains critical:* "It's Like . . . Businesses Built on Metaphors Still Need Value," Scott McNealy, *Forbes ASAP*, p. 47.

92 *Desirable attributes of charities:* Interior Army survey, April 2000, by SWR Worldwide.

95 *William Booth's funeral:* Roy Hattersley, *Blood and Fire: William and Catherine Booth and Their Salvation Army* (Doubleday, 1999), p. 435.

95 *Evangeline Booth was the single most important weapon:* Diane Winston, *Red-Hot and Righteous: The Urban Religion of The Salvation Army* (Harvard, 1999), p. 243.

96 *A public figure and newsmaker:* Ibid.

98 *Salvationists made it clear:* Ibid., p. 182.

102 *Even if you work for a good company:* Rebecca Gardyn, "Who's the Boss," *American Demographics,* September, 2000, p. 55.

102 *Buying into the organization's core principles:* "Whether or not it feels good," wrote Rebecca Gardyn in the above *American Demographics* story, "most businesses can't argue with the bottom line." In a Watson Wyatt Worldwide study, Gardyn cites, "Companies with highly committed employees have a 112 percent three-year total return to shareholders compared with a 76 percent return for companies with low employee commitment . . . Trust and confidence in senior management are the key drivers of employee commitment. In fact, employees who had high trust and confidence in their senior managers had a three-year total return to shareholders of 108 percent, compared with a 66 percent return at companies with low trust and confidence levels."

103 *Talented employees need great managers:* Marcus Buckingham and Curt Coffman, *First, Break All the Rules: What the World's Greatest Managers Do Differently* (Simon & Schuster, 1999), pp. 11–12.

103 *Massaging the values into the essence of the organization:* James C. Collins and William C. Lazier, *Beyond Entrepreneurship: Turning Your Business into an Enduring Great Company* (Prentice Hall, 1992), p. 6.

104 *Traders who tried to manipulate those rules:* Bill Atkinson, "Local Banker to Be Leader of Nasdaq," *Baltimore Sun,* May 10, 1996, p. 1C.

104 *Nasdaq is all about mutually advantageous transactions:* Al Berkeley, "Win-Win-Winnowing Out the Gamers," *Forbes ASAP,* October 2, 2000, p. 63.

105 *Having integrity turns out to be one of the most practical habits:* Al Berkeley interview with Ben Brown for "A Pioneer of the High-Tech Frontier," *Southern Living* (Mid-Atlantic edition), December, 1999, p. 16.

105 *Embody the principles you say you stand for:* Iain Somerville and John Edwin Mroz, "New Competencies for a New World," *The Organization of the Future,* p. 67.

Chapter 5

120 *An organization is like a living organism:* Arie de Geus, *The Living Company: Habits for Survival in a Turbulent Business Environment* (Harvard Business School, 1997), p. 10.

110 *Booth's first trip to the United States:* Edward H. McKinley, *Marching to Glory: The History of The Salvation Army in the United States, 1880–1980* (Harper & Row, 1980), p. 30.

111 *The life span of most organizations:* According to "most surveys of corporate births and deaths," says Arie de Geus, the former Royal Dutch/Shell executive, "the average life expectancy of a multinational corporation—Fortune 500 or its equivalent—is between 40 and 50 years. . . . A full one-third of the companies listed in the 1970 Fortune 500, for instance, had vanished by 1983—acquired, merged, or broken to pieces." (*The Living Company,* p. 1)

112 *The learning organization:* Peter M. Senge, *The Fifth Discipline: The Art & Practice of the Learning Organization* (Currency Doubleday, 1990), p. 14.

115 *"I really surrendered":* Michael Roland interview with Ben Brown.

132 *Running a successful charrette:* Andres Duany interview with Ben Brown.

Chapter 6

136 *Salvation Army major in Ohio:* Mary West interview with Ben Brown.

140 *A new hero with a new vision:* Peter Senge calls this "the myth of the hero-leader." The only problem is, says Senge, "the myth of the hero-leader creates a reinforcing vicious spiral of dramatic changes imposed from the top, and diminished leadership capacity in the organization, leading eventually to new crises and yet more heroic leaders. Worshiping the cult of the hero-leader is a surefire way to maintain change-adverse institutions. In fact, one can hardly think of a better way to achieve precisely this goal." (*The Dance of Change: The Challenges to Sustaining Momentum in Learning Organizations,* pp. 11–12)

147 *Program helps students prepare for ACT exam:* Jo Bright interview with Ben Brown.

155 *A manager is a dependable plodder:* Buckingham, Coffman, *First Break All the Rules,* p. 63.

157 *Network of autonomous divisions:* Don Fites interview with the authors.

Chapter 7

160 *Assistance in 1999:* 1999 Salvation Army Annual Report.

164 *Flood relief and restoration in 1999:* 1999 Salvation Army Annual Report.

167 *Financial management approaches:* This is one of Peter Drucker's "new paradigms" for management: "Instead of searching for the right organization, management needs to learn to look for, to develop, to test *the organization that fits the task.*" (Drucker's emphasis) (*Management Challenges for the 21ˢᵗ Century,* pp. 16–17)

167 *Emergency financial management:* David Dalberg interview with Ben Brown.

171 *Companies equate innovation with risk-taking:* Hamel, Prahalad, *Competing for the Future,* p. 313.

178 *Switching strategies to respond to new realities:* Bowden interview with Ben Brown.

Chapter 8

187 *The difference between recklessness and courage:* Ross Perot interview with the authors.

189 *Proactivity:* Covey, *The 7 Habits of Highly Effective People,* p. 71.

190 *Opportunity-seeking companies:* Hamel, *Leading the Revolution,* p. 57.

191 *It's better to make a bad decision:* Collins, Lazier, *Beyond Entrepreneurship,* p. 13.

194 *City life was inherently unnatural:* McKinley, *Marching to Glory,* p. 89.

195 *Successful farming required skill:* Ibid., p. 93.

196 *Urban life on a massive scale was here to stay:* Ibid., p. 89.

196 *The problems of city poverty:* Ibid., p. 93.

196 *Urban religion:* Winston, *Red Hot and Righteous: The Urban Religion of The Salvation Army.*

197 *Organized abandonment:* Drucker, *Management Challenges of the 21ˢᵗ Century,* p. 74.

199 *Government as a paymaster:* Peter Drucker in interview with the authors.

201 *Round-trip business:* "Peak Performance," Ben Brown, *Breakaway,* WSJ, September 27, 1999, p. 10.

203 *The responsibilities of leaders:* Drucker interview with the authors.

Chapter 9

207 *The challenges are enormous:* Interview with Kenneth Hodder.

208 *Flow and productive transcendence:* Mihaly Csikszentmihalyi, *Flow: The Psychology of Optimal Experience* (Harper & Row, 1990), p. 42 in paperback edition.

210 *Paying The Salvation Army to experience the joy of service:* Marlene Klotz Collins with Ben Brown.

213 *Work is an important part of life:* Brewer reference from interview and Chapter 2.

213 *To experience the sheer joy:* Collins, Porras, *Built to Last*, p. 70.

213 *Core values:* Core Values of Perot Systems Corporation. Taken from the website <perotsystems.com>.

214 *Dedication from employees:* Ross Perot interview with the authors.

215 *Business Strategies forecast:* Stuart Crainer, *The Management Century: A Critical Review of 20th Century Thought & Practice* (Jossey-Bass, 2000), p. 219.

215 *Polling new-tech, free-agent thinkers:* "Fast Forward: Fast Company/ Roper Starch Survey," Keith H. Hammonds, *Fast Company,* March, 2001, pp. 113–120.

216 *Knowledge workers have mobility:* Drucker, *Management Challenges of the 21st Century*, p. 21.

216 *Working life retains a strong element of security:* Crainer, *The Management Century*, p. 219.

217 *Managers become agents of the members:* Charles Handy, "Unimagined Futures," *The Future of the Organization*, p. 383.

220 *Compensating musicians with the pleasure of performance:* Rory Partin interview with Ben Brown.

223 *My faith is a relationship with Christ:* CNN.com <cnn.com/2001/ Career/Trends/02/22/nyphil.trumpet/index.html>.

SOURCES

Booth, William. *In Darkest England and the Way Out* (Tyler & Company, U.S. edition, 1942).

Brook, Stephen. *God's Army: The Story of The Salvation Army* (Channel 4 Books, Great Britain, 1998).

Cimino, Richard, and Don Lattin. *Shopping for Faith: American Religion in the New Millennium* (Jossey-Bass, 1998).

Collier, Richard. *The General Next to God* (Fontana/Collins, 1965, 1976 paperback).

Collins, James C., and William C. Lazier. *Beyond Entrepreneurship: Turning Your Business into an Enduring Great Company* (Prentice Hall, 1992).

Collins, James C., and Jerry L. Porras. *Built to Last: Successful Habits of Visionary Companies* (HarperBusiness, 1994; paperback, 1997).

Coutts, Frederick. *Bread for My Neighbour: The Social Influence of William Booth* (Hodder and Stoughton, London, 1978).

Covey, Stephen R. *The 7 Habits of Highly Successful People* (Simon & Schuster, 1989).

Crainer, Stuart. *The Management Century: A Critical Review of 20th Century Thought & Practice* (Jossey-Bass, 2000).

Csikszentmihalyi, Mihaly. *Flow: The Psychology of Optimal Experience* (Harper & Row, 1990).

de Geus, Arie. *The Living Company: Habits for Survival in a Turbulent Business Environment* (Harvard Business School, 1997).

Drucker, Peter F. *Management Challenges for the 21st Century* (Harper-Business, 1999).

Drucker, Peter F. *Peter Drucker on the Profession of Management* (Harvard Business Review, 1963).

Hamel, Gary. *Leading the Revolution* (Harvard Business School, 2000).

Hamel, Gary, and C.K. Prahalad. *Competing for the Future* (Harvard Business School, 1994; 1996 in paperback).

Hattersley, Roy. *Blood and Fire: William and Catherine Booth and Their Salvation Army* (Doubleday, 1999).

Hesselbein, Frances, Marshall Goldsmith, and Richard Beckhard, editors. *The Organization of the Future* (Jossey-Bass, 1997).

McKinley, Edward H. *Marching to Glory: The History of The Salvation Army in the United States, 1880–1980* (Harper & Row, 1980).

Peters, Thomas J., and Robert H. Waterman, Jr. *In Search of Excellence: Lessons from America's Best-Run Companies* (Warner Books, 1982).

Sandall, Robert. *The History of The Salvation Army* (Thomas Nelson and Sons, 1947).

Senge, Peter M. *The Dance of Change: The Challenges to Sustaining Momentum in Learning Organizations* (Currency Doubleday, 1999).

Senge, Peter M. *The Fifth Discipline: The Art & Practice of the Learning Organization* (Currency Doubleday, 1990).

Winston, Diane. *Red-Hot and Righteous: The Urban Religion of The Salvation Army* (Harvard, 1999).

INDEX